# Also by Ashley Ledigo

## For Children

Emajen

Dan and Min and the Missing Z

## For Adults

Fragile Lives

Be Content – Life in Shades of Grey

# EMAJEN II

# SADDLER'S TALE

**Ashley Ledigo**

LEDIGO BOOKS

# Copyright

EMAJEN II
SADDLER'S TALE



Cover Design Anthony Costin



Print ISBN: 978-1-7385587-3-5
For questions or comments about this book,
please contact the author at natorqua2024@gmail.com

For Romy

You can't as yet imagine the magic you bring to all our lives. I hope one day, when you read this, that it brings a little magic to yours...

"above all, watch with glittering eyes the world around you because the greatest secrets are always hidden in the most unlikely places. Those who don't believe in magic will never find it." — Roald Dahl

# CONTENTS

# PROLOGUE

Destiny and Anthony sat together on the grass in the late May sunshine. The half term holiday was just about to begin, and they were waiting for Destiny's mum to arrive to pick them up from school. The grass was warm and soft to the touch; Destiny ran her fingers through the delicate green fronds, lost in thought.

"Penny for them?" said Anthony.

Destiny glanced up and returned his easy smile.

"I know it's really not long at all…" she began.

"But," said Anthony. "I know exactly what you're going to say. We haven't heard from Saddler, and you thought we might have by now."

"It's silly, I know." A small frown puckered Destiny's forehead. "It just feels as though everything finished very suddenly and, now, we seem to be completely out of the loop."

"I know how you feel." Anthony gave her an understanding look. "I just think we need to be patient. There must be an awful lot to do on Emajen to set things right again!"

For a while, the pair of them sat in silence, both remembering the incredible events of a mere few months ago…

***

Everything had really begun when Destiny and her mum had gone on a riding holiday at a ranch in America. As it turned out, Destiny's mum knew the owner, who had a son of similar age to Destiny. His name was Anthony. The two children had formed an immediate bond; not least because they both had (though in different ways) tremendous empathy with animals.

The next Christmas, Anthony and his dad had gone to visit Destiny and her mum in England and, as a treat, they had all gone to a well-known Christmas horse show. It was here that the children were accosted by a rather red-faced chap, who introduced himself as Saddler. He told them that he desperately needed their help.

It had been a most bizarre meeting and what followed was, frankly, weirder still. Saddler had announced that he would, '…meet you in the green'ouse. Tonight. Twelve o'clock,' which had caused quite a lot of hilarity between the two children on the way home from the show. Nonetheless, they had been intrigued enough to creep out of the house and down Destiny's garden, to the 'green'ouse', in the middle of the night, even though neither of them believed for one minute that this strange Saddler character would actually be there.

He was.

And that's how the most unbelievable, incredible set of events unfolded, leading Destiny and Anthony into an epic adventure to save an amazing world called Emajen.

It was here they had learnt about yet another world, called Doodland, where all the doodles that humans carelessly sketch spring to life as Creations. It had been seized by a cruel and ruthless Creation called Crevitos, who had wreaked havoc and devastation on Doodland, renaming it Doomland.

But one world conquered was not enough. Crevitos knew there were other worlds; and one in particular that he was hell bent on capturing was Emajen.

When things began to go awry on Emajen, it was Saddler who used a special gateway between worlds to visit Earth. His mission was to find the right someone who might help him to save Emajen from Crevitos's dastardly designs. Crevitos had discovered Emajen's strength and yet also its weakness. The whole of that world was kept in balance and harmony by the magical Natorqua, a herd of beautiful hybrid cat-horses. Somehow Crevitos had begun to poison them in both mind and body. As the herd slowly died, Emajen was dying too. And so it was, on his travels to a ranch in America, that Saddler discovered Anthony and Destiny, and observed their incredible empathy with animals.

Without quite knowing how it had happened, the two children had become embroiled in a quest to find the Natorqua; connecting with the herd was the only way to defeat Crevitos and save Emajen from the same fate as Doomland.

The children had met some strange and wonderful beings, including Nebiré a mystic with tremendous mind-power, and Boff, a strange little fellow, who had escaped from Doomland and Crevitos's tyranny.

Destiny, Anthony, Boff and Saddler had set off together on what had promised to be an epic journey, fraught with danger and full of the most fantastic experiences. Despite the many setbacks they encountered, by far the worst had been when Saddler had mysteriously disappeared. The others had continued the journey without him, not knowing whether they would ever see him again…

***

Back in the present day, Destiny shook herself out of her reverie as her mum's car pulled into the drive. It seemed so peculiar to think that her mum knew nothing about Emajen or Doodland, or all the adventures she and Anthony had shared.

"I just hope Saddler gets in touch soon," she murmured as they climbed into the rear seats of the car.

Anthony gave her hand an affectionate squeeze and said comfortingly, "I'm sure he will."

***

It may just have been coincidence - though of course with Emajen and its inhabitants, one could never take anything for granted - but that very night there were rattling sounds of small stones against the children's bedroom windows, and when two sleepy heads emerged from their respective rooms, there was Saddler beaming cheerily up at them.

He had come to take them back to Emajen.

# CHAPTER ONE
# REUNION

*Crevitos paced. He was alone in his exile, but it wouldn't be for long - he'd make certain of that!*

*It was unthinkable that he'd been thwarted from conquering Emajen. So many months - no, years - preparing for victory, only to be beaten by what? A ragged band of nobodies! To be fair, he'd underestimated Saddler, but Saddler alone would not have been able to save his beloved world. No, it was those two meddling children from Earth who'd done the most damage. Earth, thought Crevitos, had not been on his radar, until those two brats had interfered with his plans. Well, it was on his radar now...*

It was surreal, to say the least, to be sitting once again upon those large, brightly coloured cushions, gazing in awe at the multitude of gently tinkling crystals that hung from the ceiling in Nebiré's woodland home.

Destiny and Anthony glanced at each other. Their identical expressions of slight disbelief melted away into almost perfectly matching grins. They both relaxed. Instantly, it was as if everything had slotted back into place, and it seemed the most natural thing in the world to be back on the strange and wonderful world called Emajen, on this fine, warm spring afternoon.

Nebiré, as mysterious as ever, sat gently wheezing in her great padded wicker chair. Saddler busied himself with the kettle and the tea things, humming softly to himself. In fact, it was so much like the first time Destiny and Anthony had visited Nebiré, it was almost impossible to imagine all the incredible events that had happened in the meantime.

On Earth, it was early summertime. Back then, it had been cold December, when Destiny and Anthony had found themselves plunged into the most bizarre adventure involving this world and their own.

Saddler had finished tinkering with the kettle and now emerged from the depths of the hearth with a tray of mugs: he also carried the inevitable plate of cakes and biscuits that Anthony and Destiny had come to expect as a normal part of the generous hospitality everywhere on Emajen.

"The others should be 'ere in a tick," said Saddler. His homely face, bright and cheerful as always, bore no easily discernible trace of the trials and trauma he had been through just a few short months ago. Although, thought Destiny as she watched him place the tray carefully on the table next to Nebiré's chair, there was a shadow that hadn't been there before.

No one who had not known Saddler before the 'Battle of Emajen' (so called because it was the only battle ever in Emajen's long and peaceful history) would be aware of anything amiss.

Destiny, however, thought she detected a slight wariness behind Saddler's easy smile. Perhaps she was just imagining it!

Just at that moment, Saddler turned and glanced at her as though reading her thoughts. As he did so, his hand raised involuntarily to touch a small scar just below his left eye, along the cheek bone. Destiny shivered. The moment passed as, beaming, Saddler handed Destiny a steaming mug of the nutty-flavoured tea she remembered so well.

As she smiled her thanks, three very familiar characters appeared in the entrance, The Prof, Boff and Squib. All at once, the room was energised as people exclaimed and hugged; the air was full of the joy and excitement that only reunions can bring. More tea was brewed. Nebiré, having heaved her bulk out of the chair with all four of her sturdy arms, resettled herself once more and places were found for everyone to sit. Once seated however, the Prof, eyes twinkling from beneath his bushy eyebrows, immediately leaped up again.

He struck himself dramatically on the forehead. "What a dunderhead," he chuckled. Raising one of those impressive eyebrows comically at Destiny, he beckoned her to follow. Destiny looked at him quizzically, before understanding dawned upon her, and she fairly flew down the dimly lit corridor to the hillside entrance.

Sure enough, in the woodland glade, a small, stocky black horse, as shaggy as the Prof himself, munched peacefully on the sweet, fresh spring grass.

"Kaz!" shrieked Destiny.

The horse (or nator, as such creatures were called on Emajen) lifted his head and whickered delightedly. He suffered the indignities of being hugged and kissed all over, as Destiny flung her arms around his neck. Then he snuffled hopefully around her pockets, sure she would not have forgotten to bring him a treat or two. Destiny, who now had her own pony back on Earth, rarely went anywhere without a pocketful of pony nuts, and Kaz's snufflings were soon rewarded.

"You took your time coming back to see us," sighed Kaz, rather belatedly remembering to be grumpy. Destiny laughed and rubbed his ear affectionately.

"You are a dear," she soothed. "But you know I can't do much about the time difference between here and Earth."

"Humph," said Kaz noncommittally, whilst at the same time nuzzling her ear and huffing softly through his nose at her.

"I suppose you'll be wanting me to come and hear what happened when you got home after your adventures here on Emajen!" Kaz rolled his eyes rather over-dramatically and looked sadly at the luscious grass waving softly around his hooves.

"You know we do!" said Destiny, giving him yet another hug and rifling in her pocket for yet another treat.

"But," she added more seriously, "It's Saddler's story we all need to hear. I don't think we can even begin to imagine what happened to him."

Kaz followed Destiny back through the arched doorway and along the main passageway, where the others were excitedly catching up on events. He stood in the wide entrance to Nebiré's main room, shifting his weight so that one back leg rested comfortably on the front of its hoof. Destiny plumped down on her big, soft cushion, whilst the others made a fuss of Kaz.

Then there was a moment's silence.

"Well," said Saddler cheerily, "Before I tell my story, perhaps it's about time you young'uns told us the story about what 'appened when you got back to Earth."

Anthony looked at Destiny.

"You tell it," she said.

# CHAPTER TWO
# THE RETURN HOME

*It was wonderful to see everyone again, thought Nebiré. They had been through such troubled times together when Emajen was under threat from Crevitos. Nebiré smiled to herself. She had been part of Emajen since almost forever. No one, not even she, knew how old she was. She was glad that she had been able to play her part in saving Emajen, by giving Anthony and Destiny the potion for freezing time on Earth so that they could undertake the journey to find the Natorqua. Nebiré gave an involuntary shudder. It had been a very risky thing to do, and things could have turned out very differently…*

It's not actually all that exciting," said Anthony ruefully, "Although for a while there we thought we were going to be in deep trouble!"

Destiny nodded. "When that last grain of sand fell through the egg timer, I really thought we were done for!" Then she grinned at Boff. "The last thing I heard was you saying: 'Hey, Destiny, thanks for my tartan shorts.' Then suddenly we were back in the greenhouse at the bottom of my garden."

"What's a greenhouse?" piped up Squib, pushing a lock of dark, unruly fringe out of his eyes. As always, his small, elfin-like features were full of curiosity; his young (and for many years education-starved) brain was a greedy sponge for any and all information there was to be had. The Prof, who had – in a way – adopted Squib some while back, and brought him back to Emajen, smiled affectionately and said, "I'll tell you all about greenhouses later, lad."

This seemed to satisfy Squib, who continued to absorb the situation with rapt concentration.

"Have you always known it was me who created you?" asked Destiny, looking inquisitively at Boff. The small light bulbs that surrounded Boff's translucent head, flashed as he considered the answer to Destiny's question. Drawn by Destiny when she was around seven years old, he had quickly come to life on Doodland, where so many human doodles begin their existence. Doodland, of course (or Doomland as it had been renamed) was where all the trouble had begun. It was where the cruel and ruthless Creation, Crevitos, had been let loose to wreak havoc and devastation by his young human creator.

A mere few months before, Anthony and Destiny had known nothing about other worlds. They hadn't even dreamed of a world where doodles, carelessly scribbled by human beings, actually came to life. And they would certainly still be going through their daily lives totally unaware of all of this, had Crevitos not hungered for the conquest of more than one world and set his sights on Emajen.

Boff smiled his cheeky, triangular smile. "Not to begin with," he answered. "Everyone on Doodland knows they're the creation of somebody out there…" He waved his arms in a general expansive gesture of outthereishness. "But we don't know exactly who or where. I felt like it must be so the first time I met you though. It sort of felt right."

Boff and Destiny exchanged fond looks, so eerily similar that everyone laughed. Then they all settled down again and Anthony continued with his story.

They had left Earth, he told the group, from Destiny's greenhouse on a chilly Sunday afternoon. (For some bizarre reason, Destiny's greenhouse was where Saddler had arranged to meet them, in the middle of the night, the very first time he took them through a gateway to Emajen.) They had used a time freezing potion of Nebiré's making, that would hopefully give them the time to complete their quest without anyone on Earth missing them. Anyone who knew Nebiré had absolute confidence in her powers, yet freezing time on Earth was a huge ask. Nebiré herself could not be one hundred percent sure how successful the potion would be. The children had been given a timer, which they had hoped would warn them, before the potion wore off, when they needed to return to Earth. It had run out mere seconds before they stepped back through the gateway, so what they couldn't know, when they arrived back on Earth, was whether time had totally restarted, or if there were any overlap which would enable them to get back up to Destiny's house undetected.

As Destiny had already said, they had arrived back in the greenhouse at the exact time on the very Sunday afternoon that they had left it, courtesy of Saddler's pretty, but otherwise seemingly unremarkable wooden box. A box that also happened to be a gateway between worlds.

Quite how many of these gateways existed, it was impossible to be certain, although Saddler's was one of four boxes they definitely knew about. Boff, of course, had found one in the mines of Doomland, which had enabled him to escape from there to Emajen. The Prof had his own, although no one had ever thought to ask how he had come by his - a question for another day perhaps.

Then of course there was Crevitos; but his gateway had been stretched and expanded for his own evil purposes, which had resulted in the one and only battle of Emajen. Did his gateway even still exist? Did he? These were questions that lay buried in all their minds.

As Anthony continued to set the scene for his listeners, the room seemed to darken slightly. Anyone watching from outside, would have seen Nebiré weaving her magic, with long, tapered fingers, creating a visual replay that made everyone in the room begin to feel as though they had travelled back in time and were watching events unfold from afar…

***

Although it had been autumn on Emajen, it was still relatively warm there. On Earth, in Destiny's greenhouse on a crisp, December afternoon, the watery sun did little to dispel the chill in the air. Destiny shivered, glad that she had grabbed her jacket before they had originally set off for Emajen. It was really hard to get your head around the fact that, actually, no time at all had elapsed on Earth, between the time Anthony and she had left home, and now. She had lost count of the days they had spent travelling through Emajen (especially given the false start at the beginning of their quest) but it felt like weeks. Now they were back where they had started. It was all very disorientating. Anthony's expression suggested that he was feeling pretty much the same way. They stood for several moments, the pair of them, trying to adjust to a very different reality to the one they had just left.

Finally, Anthony shook his head, as though to nudge himself awake. Touching Destiny lightly on the arm, he said, "We need to think what to do – what to say. We need to think quickly."

Destiny struggled to pull all her thoughts together. "We don't know if Mum, Dad and Grandad are awake yet, or what they think has happened if they are."

"We could try creeping up to the house to see if we can hear anything..."

"And if we get caught, what explanation would we give? We're not going to look at all suspicious, are we?"

Anthony could see what Destiny meant. "I guess you're right."

As he said this, his gaze wandered to the corner of the greenhouse, where two badminton rackets rested rakishly against the glass. "Suppose," he said thoughtfully, "we just happened to be knocking around with the rackets in the garden? That would explain why we're not in the house."

"In the middle of winter? It's freezing! They'll think we've lost our marbles or something."

"Better than thinking we just tried to poison your granddad!"

"But how would we explain the fact that the last thing your dad saw when he woke up was us standing over Granddad, with you tipping something into his open mouth?"

"I dunno – we'll have to figure that part out. What I do know is, we may not have much time. If everything's back to normal, we need to be where they can find us."

Grabbing the rackets and a stray shuttlecock from the shelf, they both hurried out of the greenhouse. Peering out from behind the row of trees that sheltered it, they could see no one watching from the kitchen window. Swiftly, they ducked around the shed and began to bat the shuttlecock backwards and forwards between them.

"Let's hope no one has been looking for us already," said Anthony, his breath visibly wafting away on a cloud of frosty air.

Destiny shivered repeatedly. "I can't hear any yelling. Maybe that's a good sign. Your dad did look pretty shocked when he woke up suddenly and saw us standing over Grandad, so if we were in trouble and they couldn't find us, there'd be yelling, right?"

"Dad doesn't really do yelling," puffed Anthony.

"Well Mum does – as you know," grimaced Destiny. "How long do you think we need to stay out here?" she grumbled. "I'm frozen. I wish I knew what was happening; not knowing is making my stomach churn…"

"I think we're just about to find out," Anthony said softly, as he bent to retrieve the shuttlecock. Striding down the garden, hands in pockets, was Anthony's dad, Matt. There was no way of telling, just by his expression, exactly what he was thinking. As he approached where they were standing, rackets in hand, looking (Destiny was certain) as guilty as hell, he took his hands out of his pockets and rubbed them vigorously together.

"Here you two young rascals are," he said cheerfully. "We were wondering where you'd got to. Can't say I much fancy it as badminton weather myself. Ready for some hot chocolate? You look as though you could do with it, Destiny." He had that incredulous what's-the-world-coming-to-youngsters-are-all-crazy-these-days expression on his face, as he turned on his heel and marched briskly back up the garden.

Sharing a glance of relief mixed with bewilderment, Destiny and Anthony both shrugged their shoulders and followed in his wake.

***

"So, you weren't in trouble then?" queried Boff anxiously.

"I don't quite understand, Anthony," mused the Prof, "How it was that your father could have observed you administering the time freezing potion to Destiny's granddad and yet not have wondered how you could be doing that and playing badminton in the garden at one and the same time?"

"That's really easy," laughed Anthony. "It was only for a split second that Dad saw us and he had just woken up suddenly from a deep sleep. He thought he'd had some amazingly bizarre dream."

"Apparently," Destiny chipped in, "Granddad then complained that he'd eaten too much and had got a horrible taste in his mouth, as well as indigestion. By the time we arrived back at the house, he'd gone upstairs to lie down with a packet of indigestion tablets."

"We all had a laugh over Dad's dream," said Anthony.

"Even if I did feel very guilty about poor old Granddad," said Destiny. "He was fine later on though and managed quite a large piece of chocolate cake for tea."

"Oh, but that's the most boring end to any story: the one people use when they can't think of anything else," the Prof said disapprovingly.

"Well, I can think of plenty of others," said Anthony mildly, "None of them very pleasant. Boring maybe, but really lucky for us."

"'Ere, 'ere," agreed Saddler.

Everyone turned to look at him. Now that Destiny and Anthony had told their story, there was another, perhaps much darker one, to be told. One that Saddler knew he had to tell. One he was not looking forward to telling. With an audible sigh, he said, "Before I start, I fink I could do wiv another cup of tea."

# CHAPTER THREE
# TYING UP LOOSE ENDS

*Crevitos was a genius. He knew it, and anyone who'd had the misfortune to have dealings with him, would definitely discover the fact sooner rather than later. Genius, unfortunately tainted by malicious lunacy. He'd heard it said more than once - even by those who were supposed to be loyal to him.*

*Although - he thought to himself as he paced his dimly lit chamber - that surely is a matter of opinion! A cruel smile played briefly across his features, to be swiftly replaced by an expression of seething disgust. Genius housed in a flimsy body created by a mere boy on this Earth place! For a while he had fed off this Earth boy's passion for his creation, but then the boy had lost interest. Lost interest in him, Crevitos! Unbelievable. Yes, it had left him free to conquer Doodland, but it had also left him without the vital strength and power that he needed in order to be a great multi-world ruler. It had left him too reliant on others.*

*Nevertheless - here, the mean smile flickered to life once more - true genius would always find a way…*

Fresh mug of tea in hand, Saddler sat on a high-backed wooden chair, next to the table which housed Nebiré's mystical array of bottles and phials of all shapes and sizes. As he lifted his mug to sip his tea, something glinted on his little finger. Destiny gasped.

"The ring, Saddler. The one the Prof gave me. That's part of your story, isn't it?"

Saddler nodded slowly and looked at the Prof who was seated in an armchair across the room.

"I've some'ow never found the right time to thank you," said Saddler gravely. "What power it 'ad, is gone now for sure, but it saved my life and probably the 'ole of Emajen wiv it." Standing rather stiffly, he carefully set his mug down on the table and walked across to the Prof, his hand held out in front of him to shake hands. The Prof eyed him with bemusement, but only for a second, before leaping up from his chair. Standing, he was a full head and shoulders taller than Saddler, a great hairy bear of a man.

"Just grateful you're alive and well and here to tell your tale," he said gruffly. He ignored Saddler's outstretched hand and engulfed him in an enormous bear hug. Saddler emerged a few seconds later ruffled and somewhat pink about the cheeks. But somehow, a tension that had crept un-noticed into the room, had lifted. The very air itself seemed to breathe again, and the crystals high above their heads tinkled softly, as if with a sigh of relief. All at once, Saddler was bombarded with a barrage of questions from all sides: 'How did the ring save your life? Where did you go? How on Emajen did you end up leading an army against Crevitos?' and so on.

He held his hands out in front of him to ward off their eager thirst for answers and sat down on his chair once more. "I'll try to answer your questions as best I can, but it's a long story and some of it I'm not even sure *I* understand.

Nebiré who had sat quietly all this time now spoke in her deep rumbling voice. "Perhaps it would make sense for each of us to revisit where we saw Saddler last. Then he will know where to begin his story."

They all nodded in agreement, except Kaz who now appeared to be dozing with his head resting comfortably on the back of the Prof's chair. Squib, seated cross-legged on a cushion at the Prof's feet, was deftly weaving plaits into Kaz's tail. It was a heart-warming picture that made Destiny smile. Somehow it was hard to imagine how different things might have been here on Emajen if Saddler had not returned.

Anthony spoke up first. "Obviously, the last time we saw you Saddler," here he looked at Boff and Destiny who had both been with him at the time, "Was when you left us in the forest to go to town to get provisions.

At this point, it had to be explained to the others why Saddler had elected to go off on his own and why they hadn't all remained as a group. Destiny and Anthony had discussed their experiences on Emajen many, many times, yet somehow on Earth their exploits had quickly seemed to become less and less real. Re-living now, how Crevitos had managed to dupe them into believing a whole town was real, not to mention drugging them and having them locked in a cellar, made Destiny shiver at the memory.

"So, you see," Saddler was saying, "Wiv all that hallucinogenic drug still in their systems, they were in no fit state to come wiv me. Looking back, perhaps I should 'ave known better. Crevitos was obviously dead set against us reaching the Natorqua and seems 'e would do pretty much anything to stop us."

"Let me just interject here, if I may," said the Prof. "I can see the logic behind your decision, but, Destiny, what made you give Saddler the ring? As far as you knew, he would return in just a few short hours."

Destiny frowned. "You know, I'm really not sure. You gave it to me, because you said it had the power to heal and there was just something niggling at me. Maybe I thought he might – I don't know – trip over a log or bash his head on a low-hanging branch or something. It just suddenly seemed the right – no not right, important, it seemed an important thing to do, in that moment."

"Well," said Saddler wryly, "I'm jolly glad you did, or I wouldn't be 'ere now."

Next the Prof and Squib explained that they had last seen Saddler, as well as the children and Boff, the second time the group had all set off to try to track the Natorqua. Everyone knew the story of how Crevitos had tricked the travellers and played mind games with them on their first attempt.

Now though, it was Destiny's turn to pose a question: "But you and Squib turned up just after we found the Natorqua. How did you know where we'd be?"

"Ah!" The Prof smiled. "I think Nebiré might be the one to explain that."

Nebiré inclined her head in acknowledgement and her three chins wobbled gently. Her one startling purple eye regarded them all benignly as she wove her own thread into the tapestry of Saddler's unfolding story:

When Saddler had first taken Anthony and Destiny to meet Nebiré, all they had known was that she had the capacity to use a vast amount of her brain, far, far more than even the most highly intelligent person on Earth. At the time, and before they had met Nebiré, Destiny had asked why Nebiré herself could not undertake the journey to find the Natorqua, the beautiful hybrid cat-horses that were the guardians of peace and well-being on Emajen. Now as Nebiré shifted her bulk in her enormous wicker chair, Destiny remembered how Saddler had replied: "She would never make the journey."

So, as she took up telling the next thread of the story, this was what gave such significance to what Nebiré told them next. As well as, or indeed perhaps because of, Nebiré's incredible mind-power (as they called it here on Emajen) she was able to see far afield from her own forest lair: sometimes into the past; sometimes the present; and occasionally to what might be yet to come. Often images would form through her crystal web; at other times visions would appear to her as she sat in a deep trance-like state.

It was through one of these visions that she had tracked Saddler through the forest as he left the others to go in search of provisions. Although she could only see Saddler himself, she knew in every tense fibre of her being that there was another presence there. And there was something wrong with the forest too: no bird song; no scurrying of small animals; and – more worrying – no tree hum. It was this lack of tree hum that had disturbed Nebiré most in her trance-like state. Trees were rarely silent, even during the day. It was most unusual for every single part of a tree to be asleep all at the same time. She had witnessed Saddler deliberately stumble and glance behind him, so he too was aware of something or someone else there. She had seen him enter the clearing and she had not only seen, but physically felt the shove that had sent him stumbling through the cavernous hole which opened up in the trunk of the enormous tree right at the centre of the clearing.

Nebiré had snapped out of her trance and sat trembling, her heart shaped face pale and beaded with sweat. And she had known that she must, somehow, make her way to the Prof's house before she lost sight of Saddler forever.

Saddler, the Prof and Nebiré all lived within a rough triangle of each other, hence the journey from one to the other generally took around an hour or so, depending on how quickly you walked. For Nebiré though, this was a tremendous undertaking. Her girth alone made walking very far extremely tiring. Add to this the large, webbed toes that gave her a gait similar to that of a duck, or a goose, and it meant that a journey of any distance would be a great effort, to say the very least. Of course, the forest in which her under-hill home nestled adored her down to the very last leaf and blade of grass. Always ready to protect Nebiré from strangers, or to have a little fun with her friends, the trees and paths had gone out of their way to create the most direct trail for Nebiré to follow. At times, the lowest branches (where strong enough) even swept Nebiré gently off her feet and carried her carefully, one to another, as far as they could. Despite this, the journey to the Prof's house, though it was a labour of extreme urgency, had taken Nebiré most of the afternoon and she had arrived at his front door wheezing and exhausted. The Prof immediately helped her inside and installed her in the largest armchair he could find. Squib, unbidden, scurried here and there, finding cushions for her back, a bowl of soothing water for her feet and an enormous pot of tea. Although he was not of Emajen by birth, Squib had almost instantly become as much one of its inhabitants as any born there. And like most of its inhabitants, he idolized Nebiré and would do anything for her.

Hovering by the arm of her chair, he had waited patiently to see if there was anything else she might need. Once she had quite recovered, Nebiré had smiled at him, so that her one purple eye crinkled upward at the corners. It was a radiant smile, full of tenderness for this bashful, gentle slip of a boy. She patted his small hand with one of her own much larger ones.

"Thank you, Sebastian Quentin Isaiah Brown," she intoned in her deep rasping voice. "I feel much rested after all your care. Be at peace now, child, we have much to discuss."

Squib's chest had puffed out with pride. Nebiré was the only one who still used his full set of names. They were the only thing from his past that had any real significance for him, and it made him full of joy to hear them used. He sat on the floor beside her chair and gazed at her with large puppy-dog eyes, ready and willing to jump to his feet at any moment to do her bidding. Periodically, one of Nebiré's four expressive hands would ruffle his hair fondly and his whole face would light up with sheer joy. He had listened to all that she had to tell the Prof; his bright little brain missed nothing. She had explained to the Prof, what she had witnessed in her vision and how this meant that Destiny, Anthony and Boff would be left to continue the search for the Natorqua on their own.

"I have no doubt," she had rasped solemnly, "That Crevitos is behind this. I am as certain as I can be that he now has Saddler with him on Doodland. Further than that, I cannot yet see."

The Prof had been extremely concerned. "What's to be done?" he queried. "Should we try to catch up with the others? They may need all the help they can get."

"That, too, would be an excellent plan," said Nebiré. "But it's not the reason I have made the journey here today. My mind-power is strong, as you know." (This she had uttered with no sense of arrogance, just a simple statement of fact.)

The Prof nodded in acknowledgement.

"However, my mind-power is limited on other worlds, especially one in the grip of as much evil as Doodland is. What I need," she continued, "is some possession of Saddler's in order that I may make some connection with him, across the two worlds, and hopefully keep track of what is happening to him. Do you have such an item?"

The Prof stroked his beard thoughtfully and was just about to answer in the negative and suggest that perhaps he should pay a visit to Saddler's wife, when Squib appeared silently by his side. The Prof had not seen him leave, but Nebiré smiled. Her body might be slow, but her mind missed nothing. In his hands, Squib was tightly clutching a blue cap. The very one (so long ago did it seem now) that one of the trees at the bottom of the Prof's path had snagged off Saddler's head, when he and the children had visited the Prof for the very first time. Nebiré beamed widely at Squib.

"That will do very nicely," she said. Then as if reading his thoughts, she murmured: "And you have been so kind this day, such a clever young soul – is there something I can do for you in return?"

Squib had looked shyly up at the Prof, who smiled reassuringly down at him. Summoning all of his great courage, Squib asked in his fluting voice: "Please, Nebiré, may I see your other eye?"

A deep rumbling chuckle surfaced from somewhere deep in Nebiré's chest, as she answered pleasantly: "That you may."

Using all four arms to shift her weight around in the chair, she had turned so that Squib could see the back of her head. As he watched, her long, flowing hair parted to reveal an exquisite, blue eye. It, too, crinkled amiably up at the corners and he gave a gasp of admiration at its delicate beauty. Then it was gone, covered once more by Nebiré's long, thick locks.

"Thank you," breathed Squib, hugely satisfied.

"You are most welcome, Master Sebastian Quentin Isaiah Brown."

Nebiré heaved herself out of the chair. "I must set about my return journey, with as much haste as I am able. You, too, have your own journey to prepare for."

At this, the Prof grinned. "I think we can make your return journey a little quicker. Hold on a tick." So saying, he disappeared from the room, only to return moments later. He gestured at the window, saying rather grandly: "Madam, your carriage awaits."

Sure enough, at the bottom of the drive, there stood Kaz, still munching on his last mouthful of grass, but attached to the Prof's small wooden cart. Ordinarily, such was his nature, he would have moaned and groaned at the faintest suggestion of such a task as taking someone home, especially given this someone's rather broad girth. For Nebiré, however, he would gallop all the way to the end of Emajen and back, without so much as a grumble.

And so it was, with Nebiré safely (and with some difficulty) installed in the cart, Kaz had set off at a stately plod to return her to her forest home. The Prof and Squib had waved until they were out of sight and then hurried back inside to make the preparations for their own journey.

# CHAPTER FOUR
# SEEKING SADDLER

*Sitting with her companions, safe in her woodland home, the surroundings began to fade and become unreal as Nebiré's mind slipped back in time. Bodily, she was present telling her story in a sonorous voice to her beloved friends. In her mind, however, she retraced every moment of the return journey from the Prof's dwelling to her own. Her thoughts were a web of emotions. Her present-day mind knew, with total clarity, that what she was reliving was over. It was done. Emajen was safe and all her companions along with it. But her past mind knew nothing of this.*

*The fear was there.*

*It was real.*

*And yesterday, today, tomorrow, merged into a pool of disturbing memories…*

The journey back to Nebiré's house had indeed been very much quicker than the outward trip. On reaching the edge of the clearing, a huge oak tree had lifted Nebiré gently from the back of the cart and set her down with equal tenderness on the ground beside Kaz. She had made much of him, and, if nators could smile, he would most certainly have been beaming from ear to ear.

"See him back safely to the track," she had instructed the trees, giving Kaz one final pat. There was an answering rustle of leaves which seemed to satisfy her and at last she turned to shuffle through her front door, as quickly as she was able. Once inside, Nebiré had immediately set to work. There was a niggling sense of foreboding fluttering liked a trapped butterfly within her being, and she was eager to find Saddler to see how he was faring.

First, however, she crossed the room to the crystal web that sparkled and glittered in one corner. As she had done before, on many occasions, Nebiré began to weave the crystals with her long, delicate fingers. At length, a picture emerged and there, as clear as day, were Anthony, Destiny and Boff. Nebiré shut her eyes for a moment and the murmur of their voices trickled into her mind. So, she understood, Saddler had gone to find the nearest town the day before and, despite assuring the others that he would be no more than a few hours, he had not returned. Now, in the cheerless chill of dawn, Boff and the children were setting off to continue their journey without Saddler.

Despite the gravity of the situation, Nebiré had allowed herself a small smile. The children were strong. She had known from the first moment of meeting them that they would see their quest through to the bitter end, no matter what the outcome might be.

Deftly, she had worked the crystals again. Although she had not long left the Prof's house, he and Squib were already just about to leave to find Anthony, Destiny and Boff. Squib had

Nebiré's directions clutched firmly in his small hand and the Prof was just placing his battered old hat firmly on his head. More importantly, as Nebiré observed the scene, she saw Kaz come plodding into view. She watched as Squib and the Prof removed the traces that attached Kaz to the cart and knew, without having to hear their words, that Kaz was reporting her safe return home.

At length, the Prof and Squib had set forth on their journey and Kaz plodded off to his favourite field for a well-deserved mouthful or two of grass. Satisfied, Nebiré turned away from her crystal web and made her way once more towards her voluminous wicker chair. Once settled, she folded her fingers carefully around Saddler's hat, and quietly closed her eyes.

At first, Nebiré had some difficulty connecting with Saddler. Deep within her dream-like state, strange pictures swam in and out of reach of her understanding. Some were fairly clear; others were mere fragments that made no sense at all. At one point, when her vision was swathed in darkness, Nebiré was aware of pain. It was not her own, but it made her gasp, nonetheless. Then came a bitterness that touched her taste buds briefly, before transforming into a warmth that suffused her whole body. Abruptly, her thoughts cleared. Finally, there was Saddler sitting on the edge of a small bed.

The room he was in appeared to curve on all sides. It was gloomy and filled with deep shadows. As she watched, a new figure swam into view. It was tall and imposing and with a face of conflicting cruelty and beauty. It struck fear into Nebiré's very core. Inside her trance, she faltered, shrinking away from this new presence. On the outside her body shuddered with fear and loathing at what she could see. And then more images began to form, rushing through her mind like a film on fast forward: Saddler descending seemingly endless stairs; Saddler in some kind of box-like construction, plummeting deep into the bowels of Doodland; Saddler watching, sickened and horrified, as Creations underwent the most torturous process imaginable in Crevitos's attempts to create an invincible army. All that Saddler saw, Nebiré saw. All that he felt, she felt. It was a vision such as she had never experienced before. It was almost a relief when Saddler and Crevitos returned to Crevitos's room at the top of the tower.

But what happened next, Nebiré was at a loss to comprehend. For a while, Saddler and Crevitos talked, although it was unclear to her what was being said. Then suddenly, Saddler was raising a phial to his lips and Nebiré cried out a silent, helpless warning. But it was too late, she had lost him. Saddler was no more.

# CHAPTER FIVE
# INTUITION

*Being a nator (the Emajen version of a horse) Kaz had a rather different view of the world than his human / doodle / mystical companions. He was proud of the part that he had played in saving Emajen, but he didn't dwell too much on the past. In Kaz's mind, things were always as they were in the here and now. The past was gone. The future was unfathomable. As long as there was tasty grass or hay to munch and a comfy place to rest, everything was pretty much OK in his world.*

*Despite this, he knew that his friends - Saddler in particular - had suffered from the traumatic experiences they had been through when Crevitos had threatened the very fabric of Emajen.*

*And if Saddler needed solace, he, Kaz, was the one to give it. Nebiré wasn't the only one on Emajen with a little magic to offer…*

A lengthy silence filled the room. Even the crystals had stilled their usual tinkling chatter. Saddler's face had taken on an unaccustomed grimness, as though he were reliving every moment of the scenario that Nebiré painted from her vision.

At last, Destiny said quietly, "Can you bear to go through it all again, Saddler? It must have been dreadful."

Saddler looked up with a wan expression. In an attempt to brighten the glumness that seemed to have settled over the room, he said lightly, "At the very least, I fink I might need another cup of tea."

At once, both Destiny and Boff leaped to their feet (it really was incredible how eerily similar they were sometimes) and began to busy themselves with the kettle and the tea things. As if by mutual agreement, conversation began to flow on various subjects not remotely connected with Saddler or the events that had taken place some months previously.

Kaz, though apparently dozing, had strangely missed nothing at all and he now plodded across the room to where Saddler sat. With that intuition that animals often seem to possess (which, sadly, humans do not) he had gently lowered his chin onto Saddler's shoulder and was breathing warm, soothing puffs of air through his nostrils onto Saddler's cheek. By the time the tea was made, and once more distributed around the group, Saddler did seem to have lost a little of his previous paleness, and his hand was steady as he accepted his cup from Boff.

Job done, from his perspective, Kaz took himself over to Destiny where he nudged at her pocket expectantly.

Destiny laughed. "You are one cheeky nator," she said with mock severity. Nonetheless, she was touched by Kaz's concern for Saddler, and she delved into her pocket for a couple of treats.

Once everyone was settled, a hush descended on the room again as they all looked to Saddler to begin his story. At length,

Squib, who could contain his eagerness no longer, asked shyly, "Where did you go Saddler, when Nebiré lost you in her dream?"

Saddler smiled fondly down at the young lad, and although it was clearly a very hard thing to do, he finally began his tale.

# CHAPTER SIX
# SADDLER'S STORY - THE BEGINNING

*Within his self-imposed exile, Crevitos thought long and hard. It was vitally important for him to understand everything - every nuance of what had transpired to bring about his defeat, so that he had ended up here.*

*Often his reflections turned to Saddler. Saddler, for whom he had had high hopes. The potion Crevitos had given Saddler should have completely wiped Saddler's mind of his whole past. At the time, Crevitos had been convinced that it had. Now, it was clear that that simply could not have been the case. Something had blocked Saddler's mind from being entirely erased, and something had brought Saddler's memories flooding back again. Somehow, sometime, he, Crevitos, was going to find out what…*

On reflection, Saddler thought that his very first memory of being on Doomland was that of feeling the ring in his trouser pocket. The ring was small and smooth and rather cold. Of course, at that point, he didn't know that he had trousers, or a pocket, or indeed anything at all, since his memory had been virtually wiped clean by the potion Crevitos had induced him to swallow. However, as he closed his fingers around the ring, he could feel the way that it coiled around in a circle. Absently, he traced this coil with his thumb and, as he did so, felt something shift within his brain. All this of course he now understood, but at the time, he was just aware of things. Aware in the same way that a baby begins to learn and process information, which it will better understand as it grows up.

To begin with, there was dark and light (though not very much light up in Crevitos's high tower room) and things that seemed to happen quite regularly, like food and drink. Crevitos was there often, his cruel smile evident every time Saddler perfected a new skill. (Some of these tasks were things that Saddler shuddered to remember!) And Saddler learned fast; his mind was like a sponge, eager to absorb as much information as it could possibly get. He learned fast because his mind was like a sponge, but he also learned fast because somewhere deep within the recesses of both his body and mind there were memories of actions he had performed before.

He learned fast because of all these things, but he learned faster still, because when he had taken the potion that Crevitos had offered him, he had slipped his hand into his pocket and simultaneously rubbed the ring from its jewelled snake's head to its coiled tail. The ring had responded quickly, immediately sending energy into Saddler's body, to release his own endorphins. These fought valiantly within him to reject the effects of the potion, which threatened to obliterate Saddler's very existence. For a moment or two, the two battling forces warred within Saddler, but the potion was strong, and it would have its way.

What Crevitos didn't know, couldn't know (perhaps would never know) was that the ring spent much of its power helping Saddler's own body to protect his mind from being completely erased. So, for Crevitos, the fact that Saddler responded so well and so quickly to his teaching, was a triumph. He might not have been quite so elated had he known about the ring, or the fact that there was still a little – although not much –power left within it.

Then came a day when Crevitos took Saddler out of his gloomy eyrie and led him down many stone steps to another room, larger and airier than his own. Something about the trip down the stairs seemed familiar to Saddler, as though he had been there before, but the effort of placing one foot a whole step lower than the other, soon commanded all his attention.

Crevitos watched with wry amusement as Saddler placed his right foot carefully on the step below him and followed it cautiously with his left. Until now, Crevitos had been extremely patient with Saddler, no matter how small or basic the task he needed to learn. This time, however, there was a slight terseness in Crevitos's voice as he said, "One foot after the other, like this, otherwise it will take us all day just to get down the stairs."

Saddler had watched dutifully as Crevitos bounded lightly down the steps and disappeared around a bend out of sight. Anxious not to be left behind, Saddler had tried, warily at first, alternating his feet as he made his way down the stairs. After a few halting steps, his muscles appeared to remember what they were supposed to do, and he even tried a couple of light skips that brought a smile of pleasure to his face.

Around the bend, Crevitos heard Saddler's quickened footsteps and he smiled his mocking smile. As Saddler rounded the corner, Crevitos flung open a stout wooden door to his left.

"Welcome to your new abode," he smirked.

At first, the brightness hurt Saddler's eyes, accustomed as he had been to the gloom of Crevitos's room. Then, as his eyes adjusted themselves to the light, he looked around with delight. Everything from the large, soft four-poster bed to the tall, imposing windows fascinated him, and he mumbled unintelligible sounds of discovery to himself, as he explored the room.

Crevitos raised an eyebrow and left Saddler to it, closing and locking the door softly behind him.

# CHAPTER SEVEN
# NEW BEGINNINGS

*Although Nebiré had not been able to see all that had happened to Saddler in her visions, she had seen enough. She had never fully disclosed to anyone, especially not Saddler, how much she had witnessed of his 'rebirth' on Doomland, but it had been almost as painful for her to helplessly watch what he went through there as the retelling of it must be for him now.*

*To begin with, she had not known about the ring in his pocket, or about the powers it possessed that had protected him from Crevitos's mind-erasing potion. It had soon become obvious to her, though, that there were certain things Saddler was keeping from Crevitos. At the time it had given her a faint flicker of hope…*

Having explored every inch of the room, gazed out of the window for several minutes (not that there was much to see but a barren wasteland) and bounced, somewhat clumsily, on the four-poster bed, Saddler had soon sampled all the delights his new living space could offer.

His brain, having made light of the more mundane things it was expected to learn, was now feeling pretty starved of stimulation. This being the case, when Crevitos next entered the room, Saddler had curled himself up in a tight ball in one corner and refused to even acknowledge that Crevitos was there.

Crevitos, as always, was highly amused. He was finding Saddler's retraining both a challenge and a great source of entertainment. Although he was impatient to have Saddler ready for the job of drawing Creations, his scientists – though frustratingly close – had not yet finalised the way to create an army-sized gateway between worlds. Moulding Saddler's brain to his own personal specifications was a welcome diversion, which helped to keep Crevitos's impatience at bay.

Now he looked at Saddler's curled up form and knew it was time for the next phase in his plan.

"If you are good," he said, in his silkiest voice, "I have a new toy for you." So saying, Crevitos turned swiftly and left the room.

Moments later he returned with an armful of objects, which he placed carefully on the bed. Selecting one from the pile, he crossed the room, sat himself comfortably in a solid wooden chair and, resting his elbows lightly on its arms, said: "Do you not want to see what I have here, Saddler?"

Saddler, who had turned his head just enough to watch Crevitos sit down, now jerked away grumpily. Crevitos could see that Saddler was interested, but that he wasn't ready to show it yet. With that familiar curl of his lip, Crevitos opened the object and began to talk, ignoring Saddler completely.

To begin with, Saddler thought that Crevitos was talking to him, so he pretended he wasn't listening. After a little while though, when the talking didn't stop, he turned his head just enough to see that what Crevitos was saying appeared to be connected to the thing that he was holding. Indeed, it would seem that Crevitos was talking to himself.

Surliness forgotten, Saddler crept closer to where Crevitos was sitting. Now, he could see that Crevitos seemed to be talking to the object, although the object itself made no noise at all. Shifting closer still, Saddler could see that the object was white with black marks on it, and something else that he recognised as looking a little bit like Crevitos himself. This was exactly what his information-starved brain needed. He was so absorbed in trying to make out what this thing was, that when Crevitos flipped a part of it noisily from one side to another, Saddler jumped out of his skin.

"Do you like my book?" Crevitos asked, making no reference to Saddler's petulant sulk in the corner of the room.

"B- b- bk?"

"Book"

"Book!"

This seemed familiar to Saddler, but even if he could have formulated the words, something would have prevented him from saying so. Crevitos went on to show him that this thing called a book had words and pictures, all of which Saddler's brain stored away for future use.

For a while, Saddler was content to spend his time looking through these objects that he now knew were called books. Periodically, Crevitos would appear and read one to him. He would show Saddler the pictures and Saddler would try out the new words that Crevitos taught him. Even though everything seemed as though it were new to Saddler, he had strange feelings as though many of these things were actually old friends.

After a time though, Saddler grew bored with the same stories and pictures, and he grew restive again. Then, Crevitos appeared in Saddler's room with a new set of objects, which he placed carefully on the bed. Intrigued, Saddler looked at Crevitos enquiringly, however Crevitos made no attempt to show Saddler what they were. He merely gave his twisted smile and left the room again.

Not entirely sure whether these objects were for him, Saddler just stood and considered them for a while. Then he moved closer and, glancing around rather furtively, stretched out his hand to touch one of the objects. He snatched it away again quickly, as though he expected the whole room to come tumbling down around him as a penance for his wickedness. However, when nothing happened, he lowered himself gently on to the bed, next to the objects, and sat looking at them thoughtfully again for a while.

At length, he could resist no longer. Picking up the first of the objects, Saddler looked at it carefully. It was about as long as his hand, from the tip of his middle finger to the start of his wrist. (He knew what these parts of his body were called now, from one of the books Crevitos had shared with him.) The object was thin, round and solid, with a pointy end, and Saddler spent quite a bit of time enjoying the smooth feeling of rolling it between his fingers. When that became boring, he sniffed at it, but it didn't smell of much. Finally – feeling by now quite frustrated with the thing – he opened his mouth and took a cautious bite. Quickly, he spat it out in disgust, noticing as he did so that there were now little marks on the object where he had bitten it. At last, here was an amusing game. Putting the object in his mouth again, he happily chomped up and down, enjoying the sensation as his teeth bit into its firm substance.

There were several of these objects on the bed – although not all exactly the same – so he spent some time trying out the different patterns he could make with his teeth on each one, until this game too lost its appeal, and he grew bored once more.

The only other object on the bed, was what appeared to be another book. Crevitos had told him it was really important to be careful with books: 'They hold the knowledge of the whole world,' he had said gravely. So, Saddler picked this one up very gently and turned the pages to see what was inside. Nothing. Page after page, there was nothing but blank white paper. Disgusted, he threw it down on the bed – only to discover that a small piece came away in his hand with a rather satisfying ripping sound. He picked the book up again, feeling a bit guilty. Maybe the books only found their words and pictures when Crevitos talked to them, and now he had broken this one.

In his clumsy attempt to squash the ripped piece back onto the page, he only succeeded in ripping it more. Finally, his irritation with the useless things that Crevitos had left him, boiled over. With total abandon, he grabbed hold of the empty book and ripped and tore at it with all his might. Soon there were small, torn shreds of white littering the bed and floor like ragged bits of confetti. This was so hugely satisfying, that once he had finished Saddler looked around to see what else he could do.

His eyes alighted on the chewed objects still lying on the bed. With a whoop of excitement, Saddler snatched them up and threw them whole-heartedly at the nearest wall. They made an interesting clatter, so he crossed the room to pick them all up to do it again. As he bent down however, Saddler noticed several strange marks on the wall that he was sure hadn't been there before.

His brain whirred. Thoughtfully, he picked one of the objects up and threw it at the wall again. Nothing happened. He tried again. Still nothing. Irritated, he tried again, harder this time. The pointy end of the object hit the wall first. There! Saddler saw with joy that there was a new mark on the wall. He tried again; this time however, he held the object firmly and jabbed the pointy end at the wall. A mark – it made a mark! His brain went into overdrive. If this object made a mark, then what about the others? They all looked sort of the same. Carefully, he tried each one and found, to his joy, that they all made marks. Some were thicker, or thinner, than others and there were several different colours (he'd learnt about colours) but they all made marks.

It was a revelation!

And so it was, that when Crevitos returned, he found Saddler happily engrossed in making a variety of lines and squiggles all over the walls of his room. Saddler's relationship with Crevitos was complicated. Although Crevitos had never (as far as Saddler's new brain could recall) been angry or unkind to him, Saddler had an instinctive dislike of Crevitos that he didn't quite understand. However, as Crevitos was the only other being he had ever come in contact with, Saddler was also keen to please.

All the good things such as the books and the food, seemed to appear when Crevitos entered the room and it gradually occurred to Saddler that maybe these things would stop if Crevitos wasn't happy. Now, as Crevitos surveyed the mess all over Saddler's room, it seemed as though this might indeed be a moment when Crevitos wasn't pleased. Saddler stood looking helplessly from the mess to Crevitos and back again. He hung his head, ashamed, not seeing the flicker of cruel amusement that crossed Crevitos's face. He did, however, hear Crevitos sigh; this was followed by the appearance of an empty box on the bed. He watched carefully as Crevitos picked up the pencils and threw them in the box. Then Crevitos gestured to the shreds of paper all over the room.

"Tidy these!" He commanded in a voice that suggested Saddler had better obey.

"Put them all in here," – he waved towards the box – "And be done by the time I return!"

So saying, he swept from the room again, leaving Saddler gazing glumly at the chaos around him. Once he began to pick up the pieces of paper though, Saddler quite enjoyed himself. Nothing had happened to him, and tidying up the mess was actually rather satisfying. When he had finished, Saddler surveyed the room and decided there were other things he could do to make it look nicer.

He spent a happy time straightening the curtains, smoothing out the covers on his bed and arranging bits and pieces as neatly and tidily as he could. This done, he waited eagerly for Crevitos to return.

At last Crevitos appeared and, for a moment, Saddler's buoyant mood faltered at the stern look on Crevitos's face. Having surveyed the neat and tidy room however, Crevitos gave Saddler one of his wry smiles.

"Excellent, excellent. At last, we are making progress."

This didn't mean a whole lot to Saddler, but he could see that Crevitos was happy. He also noticed that Crevitos had another pile of objects in his hands, which he placed once more on the bed. They were identical to those he had left before. Crevitos raised his eyebrows.

"Be more careful with these," he said firmly and then left the room once more.

# CHAPTER EIGHT
# WHO IS SADDLER?

*Never able to be still for long, Crevitos paced some more. He was still convinced that initially, in the early days after being given the potion, Saddler had genuinely lost his mind. There was no way Saddler could have faked having to relearn the very basics, from feeding himself to speaking his first intelligible words.*

*Crevitos wracked his highly intelligent brain for signs that he had missed. Was there a moment in time when Saddler had become aware of who he was and had hidden this knowledge from Crevitos? Given the circumstances, such deception was inconceivable - and yet…*

It was extremely tempting just to repeat the same actions all over again. Making a mess and marking the walls had been huge fun; something in Saddler's brain though, warned him that Crevitos might not be so easy going if he did it all again. Saddler sat down on the bed once more and considered the objects carefully. There was a reason why Crevitos had brought him these things; he needed to fathom out what that reason was. Sighing, he looked at the marks on the wall. Some of them were actually quite interesting. One or two even looked a bit like something – although he had no idea what those somethings might be.

He looked at the wall and back at the new mark-making objects on the bed. Wall – bed – wall- bed – wa… book. Book!

That was it. Saddler sat up straight, suddenly excited. The empty book, he was sure that was key. If the mark-making objects made marks on the wall, they would probably make marks on the empty pages of the book, wouldn't they? Then he slumped again, uncertainly. But supposing that was wrong. Supposing he made marks in the book and ruined it: Crevitos would definitely not be happy then. Supposing, though, that he just made marks on one page. Then he could see how Crevitos reacted, and he wouldn't have actually spoilt the whole book.

Pleased with this reasoning, Saddler chose one of the mark-making objects and carefully opened the book to its first empty page. To begin with, he tried making marks with the object clutched tightly in his fist, which was OK, but somehow didn't quite feel right. He tried holding the object in several different ways and gradually filled the page with a variety of marks; some were more, and some were slightly less clumsy. Finally, he found a way with the object grasped – not too tightly – between his thumb and first finger. Strangely, this also felt familiar, but as he didn't understand this feeling, Saddler ignored it.

Now, of course, just as he had found a better way of holding the object, the page was covered in marks, and there was no room to make any more. He turned the page over and it occurred to him that if it was already marked on one side, he couldn't make it too much worse by marking it on the other. Excitedly, he set to.

Now he found that he could control the object much more easily; moreover, he could think of a style of mark that he wanted to make and then make it. He began to look around the room and see the objects in a new light. It seemed that if you could make the right kind of marks, then you could make them look like whatever you wanted. Mostly, this was pretty unsuccessful, however a new determination to succeed gripped Saddler. Page after page (all thoughts of spoiling the book forgotten) was filled with Saddler's attempts to copy the objects in his room. Finally, he looked at the windows. Really, they were just a series of straight lines he realized. Drawing straight lines was hard, until he discovered that he could use the side of one of the other mark-making objects to help him make a much neater line. After three attempts, Saddler sat back and looked at his handiwork. Not bad. Not bad at all!

Saddler grinned to himself and, as he did so, pushed his hands comfortably into his trouser pockets. His left hand encountered the ring, still there, forgotten. Absently, his thumb traced the ring's coil from head to tail. He felt a strange, pleasurable sensation, like drawing energy instead of water from a well. Scarcely knowing what he was doing Saddler picked up a mark-making object once more. Pausing only to find an unmarked page, he began to create several new types of mark. When he had finished, he sat back and gazed at what he had created for a long time:

Saddler.

He knew what it was, and he knew what it meant. Saddler was his name. But who was he? Who was Saddler?

Just at that moment, the door handle began to turn. Without knowing why, but knowing that he must, Saddler tore the page from the book and quickly slipped it beneath his pillow.

# CHAPTER NINE
# LEARNING TO CREATE

*There was much about relearning to be a functioning human being that Saddler had found frustrating. Sometimes, when he looked back at what Crevitos had expected from him and what he'd been required to learn, he felt his whole body flush with a kind of hot wave of disgust mingled with fear.*

*On reflection, Saddler knew that he'd had no control over what Crevitos had done to him. Every logical cell in his brain told Saddler that he was not responsible for Crevitos's actions. And yet… yet… he still believed he should have done more. At times he would find himself crippled with feelings of embarrassment and an overwhelming sense of failure. True, Crevitos had failed in his attempt to conquer Emajen, but he had almost succeeded. Saddler was convinced that he should have found a way to prevent the Battle of Emajen from ever happening.*

*He felt he had betrayed his friends and badly let his world down…*

Much to Saddler's relief, it seemed that what he had done was exactly what Crevitos wanted. For a moment, as the door slowly opened, Saddler had looked aghast at the empty book and how very un-empty it was now, and he had expected the worst. But Crevitos had crowed with delight and produced more of the objects which Saddler now knew were called pencils and paper.

Along with these, Crevitos had also brought some simple pictures. He had explained to Saddler that he wanted him to copy these pictures, by looking at them and doing much the same as he had when he had drawn the window. To Saddler's half-starved brain, this seemed a most engaging exercise. To begin with, he found even the simplest of the pictures difficult to recreate. Drawing straight lines was one thing, but these pictures had all sorts of curves which were tricky to copy.

Crevitos had continued to read to Saddler and had begun to teach him how to decipher the letters and words. At one point, during one of these sessions, Saddler had absentmindedly stroked the ring in his pocket. He had felt that same surge of energy, almost like a small electric shock, and it was as though a bulb had switched on in his brain. Suddenly, the words on the page became very clear and he was able to follow the text that Crevitos had read him with ease. Once again, a little warning voice, somewhere deep inside, told him that this was something Crevitos should not yet know. So, he diligently practised the words and sentences that Crevitos gave him to read and faltered most convincingly over the more difficult words. Even so, Crevitos was extremely pleased with his progress.

"I knew you would have a strong brain and be quick, very quick," he enthused. "But you have surpassed all of my greatest hopes."

Saddler had grinned at this; he was pleased with Crevitos's praise. Yet more and more, he felt the need to hide how much he knew from Crevitos. More and more there was a feeling in the pit of his stomach, which he couldn't place, but made him feel very uncomfortable indeed.

Beneath each of the pictures that Crevitos gave Saddler to copy, there would be a few words explaining what the picture was of. Now, Saddler could read these easily, so he knew what the pictures were, but they still had very little meaning for him. A picture of a cat was as meaningless as a picture of a dragon: Saddler had no way of knowing if these things were real, since his brain had no experience of anything but the objects in his room. After many failed attempts with the copying, Saddler had discovered that he could hold the pictures, with a piece of paper over them, up against one of the windows. This meant that he could see the lines of the picture behind the blank piece of paper and this way, they were quite easy to draw over. It didn't take long for this to become too easy and, consequently, boring. But the skills that Saddler had learnt through tracing, now meant that he could draw all sorts of different lines much more easily.

Soon, he became extremely adept at copying the pictures Crevitos brought him, even the ones with much more detail. He even discovered that if you turned a picture upside-down and looked at the lines, and the spaces around the lines, instead of at the whole picture, it was possible to copy it almost exactly. Crevitos of course was delighted.

"This is progress beyond my greatest hope," he said gleefully.

Then he produced more paper and pencils. But this time, no picture to copy.

"This is what you are here for," he told Saddler sternly. "Your drawing skills have become honed to an excellent degree. Now I need you to draw for me. I need you to create pictures of beings that come from your own mind. Beings that are strong and fierce. Beings that will become the greatest fighting force EVER."

Having said this, he swept from the room, leaving Saddler dazed and bewildered. Feeling suddenly unsure of himself, Saddler looked helplessly at the paper before him. He tried to draw, but all that came out were pictures that he had copied again and again, that his brain now knew well. He realized that this was not what Crevitos wanted but could produce nothing else. Defeated, he crawled into his bed and hid beneath the covers, which is where Crevitos found him when he returned.

# CHAPTER TEN
# PAUSE FOR THOUGHT

*Nebiré was no stranger to the mystical things in life, or indeed to many things that your average being from almost any world would find outrageously bizarre. Nevertheless what had happened to Saddler, on Doomland, and within Crevitos's clutches, had shaken even Nebiré to her very core. The arrival of Destiny and Anthony, from the world of Earth, to try and help save Emajen, had been within her mystical powers to see, though the details and the outcome had remained unclear. But Saddler, almost stripped of his very essence by Crevitos's potion? That she had not foreseen. She had been helpless to forewarn him, let alone protect him.*

*An involuntary shudder rippled through her.*

*Things could have ended so very differently indeed…*

Saddler was quiet for so long that the others felt as though they were in a dream suspended on a cliff top, just waiting for the fall. No one could believe what they were hearing: Saddler with no will of his own; Saddler reacting as a small child might to its surroundings; and the shocking understanding of Crevitos's despicable plan for Saddler.

Finally, Kaz snorted, turned himself around and plodded off down the corridor, muttering that he needed some air. Saddler shook himself, as though it were difficult to bring himself back to Emajen. The strain of these memories was etched on his usually jovial face. It occurred to Destiny that this was merely the beginning of Saddler's tale. Undoubtedly there was worse to come. She wondered how he could bear to live with such awful memories; how could he live with knowing that he had so nearly become part of Crevitos's plan for universal domination? Without realizing that she was thinking out loud, Destiny said: "I wonder where Crevitos is now?" As soon as it was out, she regretted the thought, watching the way Saddler's face darkened.

"'E got away, is all I know." Saddler said darkly. "We should 'ave done for 'im during the Battle of Emajen, there and then. I won't forgive myself ever for that!"

Immediately, there was an outpouring from everyone: Saddler had done so much, he was a hero, in no way was it his fault Crevitos had escaped! Saddler merely grunted. Then he looked at Nebiré who nodded.

"Seems our time is up for a while," he said to Anthony and Destiny. "We'd better be getting you two back before anyone realizes you're not there."

He held up a soothing hand as Destiny started to protest. "Don't worry!" Here Saddler's amiable expression resurfaced once more, and he beamed kindly at Destiny. "I won't be telling any more of my story before you get back 'ere, and I'll come for you tomorrow night again, if that's alright?"

"Of course, it is," Anthony said firmly. "You must be exhausted." Here he shot a glance at Destiny, who instantly felt terrible and very selfish for wanting Saddler to continue with his story. "I'm sorry, Saddler," she said chastened. "I wasn't thinking."

"Don't be daft. I 'ate stopping in the middle of a good story meself."

Saddler held out his hand and helped Destiny to her feet. She gave him a fierce hug and he jestingly gasped for breath. Saddler was not the only one who had been through a lot in an attempt to save Emajen.

Anthony and Destiny had not even known that Emajen existed before Saddler had more or less accosted them one winter's day (some Earth months ago now) and enlisted their help. Saddler had travelled from Emajen to Earth in a desperate attempt to find the right 'someone' who could help him to save Emajen.

On a ranch in America, he had found Anthony and Destiny: Anthony with his unbelievable sympathy for horses and Destiny, who instantly attached herself to every animal she met. Saddler had been amazed, impressed and hopeful in equal measure and had set about planning how he could reach these two youngsters and see if he could persuade them to help him. The resulting quest on Emajen had been a big ask – actually, not big, VAST!

Looking back, Saddler shuddered to think of the dangers he had asked Destiny and Anthony to face on his behalf – on behalf of his world; a world they had known nothing about. And, of course, they had helped. They had found the beloved Natorqua who were being drained of their energies by Crevitos and who were gradually dying: Anthony had connected with the horse half of the Natorqua and Destiny had bonded with the cat half. Between them they had broken through the decimating spell Crevitos had cast over the Natorqua and restored the strength and energy to the herd.

Without the Natorqua's balancing and healing energies, Emajen was nothing. Without the Natorqua, Saddler would have failed in his attempt to defeat Crevitos's almost invincible army.

In short, without Anthony and Destiny, Emajen would now be a mere husk of a world – ruined beyond repair. Saddler – and Emajen – owed Anthony and Destiny their very existence. The adversities they had shared had formed an unbreakable bond between Saddler and the children – a friendship forged on trust. As far as Saddler was concerned, the children could do no wrong, so he wasn't upset by the fact that Destiny wanted to hear his story. In fact, he owed them his story after all they had been through.

Now, however it was time to return them to Earth for a while. No one (except perhaps Nebiré) quite knew how the times related on Earth and Emajen: If Nebiré said that it was time to go, then she was undoubtedly right. Having said their farewells to the others, Saddler produced the key from his pocket which would open the box that held the gateway between the worlds. The key grumbled in its now very familiar way, making Destiny laugh. She loved the key – much as she loved everything about Emajen – and gave it a gentle stroke.

"Where would we be without you?" she asked in a placating tone of voice.

"Stuck on Earth!" the key replied huffily, but its grumblings subsided, and it glowed a very pretty shade of pink.

Saddler opened the box and stepped through the now familiar ink blot that spread open before them. Destiny and Anthony followed him.

It was dark in the greenhouse, much as it had been when they had left it a few hours before. However, the sky was already showing signs of beginning to lighten, as it always did early on summer mornings.

"It's hard to remember how bizarre this all seemed the first time you came here," said Anthony. "Now it feels like we've always known you and Emajen."

With one more hug from Destiny and a handshake from Anthony, Saddler waved his farewell and disappeared back through the ink blob.

Tiredly, Anthony and Destiny wound their way back through the garden and silently through the house up to their rooms. It was a long while before either of them slept. Saddler's story had only just begun to unfold, and it was already mind-blowing. Neither of them could begin to imagine what perils he had yet to reveal.

# CHAPTER ELEVEN
# A DAY AT THE BEACH

*Destiny often wondered how different their lives might have been if she and Anthony had never met Saddler. To find out that other worlds existed and that there was a gateway you could travel through to reach them was surely the most incredible and exciting thing that could happen to anyone. Even now there were times that she felt she ought to pinch herself just to make sure it wasn't all some unbelievable dream.*

*To begin with, when she and Anthony had first visited Emajen, she had been very sceptical. She was certain that Saddler must be a devious, twisted and evil person who'd slipped her and Anthony some kind of mind-altering drug. She was sure that their whole experience of visiting Emajen must be an elaborate hoax. But as time went on it became all too clear that what was happening to them was real.*

*Sometimes, though, it was hard to reconcile the two very different realities…*

If both Anthony and Destiny seemed tired the next day, it was not remarked upon by either Destiny's mum or Anthony's dad. They had decided that since it was unusually warm for the time of year a trip to the beach was probably just the thing. Jenny had also, at one point, proposed an overnight stay in a B&B. Horrified, Destiny had been about to complain, when Anthony kicked her shin beneath the table where they were both droopily eating their breakfast.

Fortunately, Anthony's dad unwittingly saved the day.

"Sadly, we don't all get half term," he said with mock severity. "Tomorrow is the day that I need to see a man about a horse, so to speak."

Destiny shot him a brilliant smile of gratitude, which fortunately Matt mistook for her approval about the horse he was going to see: of course, he knew nothing about their nightly trips to Emajen, although Destiny thought he would really like it there. Animals were every bit as important on Emajen as the humans who lived there. She'd never heard of anyone badly treating an animal there: the whole of Emajen was in fact treated with so much more respect than here on Earth. And of course, the Natorqua were the most beautiful, kind, glorious creatures she had ever come across.

Maybe we need something like them here on Earth, she mused. But for now, just knowing that there were people here on Earth like Anthony's dad made a difference.

The reason he was over here from his ranch in America was because Anthony had heard about a very poorly treated horse which needed a huge amount of TLC to get it right. It just so happened that the timing coincided with the end of May half term at the English school Anthony and Destiny both attended. Matt had agreed to come and have a look at the horse and, if at all possible, to take it back to the ranch. As Destiny had witnessed there for herself, rehabilitating horses was what they did best; they were extremely good at it.

***

Rather surprisingly, Destiny thoroughly enjoyed their day out. They had decided to take their four-month-old Border Terrier cross Jack Russell with them to give her some much-needed socialising time with other people and perhaps even some other dogs. Having never felt sand beneath her paws before, Roley was in a state of such excitement that she kept on tumbling over herself in her rush to explore the next patch of sand.

Much to everyone's amusement, she very quickly discovered that trying to eat it just made you sneeze a lot and the look of surprise on her face almost made Destiny double up with laughter.

Then Roley discovered the wavelets that lapped continuously to and fro on the shoreline. To begin with, she scuttled away every time they came towards her, undoubtedly thinking that they were trying to chase her. Then as they receded, she barked at them furiously and chased them back to the sea, where the whole game began again.

By the time they had all built sandcastles (Matt declared that his was most definitely superior to the rest) and had an ice-cream or two, it was decided that a round of fish and chips would nicely complete the day before they headed home. Even Roley was allowed one small piece of fish as a special treat, which she gobbled down so fast it could barely have touched the sides.

It was a quiet journey home; the sea air had worked its magic on everyone. Now that the day was over, both Anthony and Destiny were wondering what revelations Saddler would have in store for them when they returned to Emajen that night. Roley, worn out by the excitement of the day, snored softly on Destiny's lap the whole way home and nobody remarked on it when both Anthony and Destiny said they were off to their respective beds not long after they'd arrived.

Matt and Jenny too were tired and as Matt had an early start the next morning, they weren't far behind the youngsters in heading up to their rooms. By ten o'clock, all was quiet in the household, and the children both slept soundly until Anthony's alarm went off at midnight. Blearily, he clambered out of bed, threw on his clothes and knocked gently on Destiny's door. When she appeared, looking every bit as sleepy as Anthony himself, they crept silently together down the stairs and out of the back door.

In the greenhouse at the bottom of the garden, Saddler, as always, was waiting for them. In no time at all it seemed, they were standing at the entrance to Nebiré's abode anxious to hear the next instalment of Saddler's tale.

# CHAPTER TWELVE
# DECISIONS ARE MADE

*Before Crevitos had been let loose by his Creator, Doodland had been an absolute peach of a world. Boff, a Creation doodled by Destiny when she was seven years old, had come alive on Doodland in the same way as so many others before and after him. Then, the sun had shone benignly down on them from a soft blue sky. The rain, of which there was always enough, but never too much, fell gently, watering and refreshing; it was something to delight in rather than to complain of. The inhabitants had lived in peace, relishing each new day and the advent of each new Creation.*

*Until, that was, the arrival of Crevitos.*

*Boff, who had not the most miniscule particle of nastiness in his whole being, simply could not fathom why anyone would want to conquer a world. And not just conquer it, but obliterate all that was beautiful and wonderful about it, subjecting all its inhabitants to the greatest suffering and humiliation possible…*

Crevitos paced high up in his gloomy tower, which overlooked the barren waste of Doomland. He strode to and fro like a caged tiger. His frustration was visible in every stride.

"I do not understand," he told himself for the umpteenth time. It brought him no nearer to the solution of his problem, and his problem was this: Saddler had made enormous strides with his learning. He had appeared to absorb, like a sponge, all that Crevitos had taught him, and he was also clearly able to reason through a puzzle such as what the pencils and paper were for. Saddler had worked hard and had quickly regained old skills. Of course, Crevitos had no way of knowing whether Saddler had been able to draw before, but he certainly showed great ability now in imitating whatever image Crevitos gave him to copy. But here was the sticking point, Saddler could copy; he could, and would, copy happily for hours on end. But he couldn't create. He couldn't do the very thing that Crevitos wanted him to do, which was to draw beings that would ultimately come alive as Creations on Doomland. (What a far superior name that was for this world than its previous title Doodland. Well, there was nothing meek and mild and fluffy about Doomland; it was a strong name for a world with a strong ruler.)

But the potion Crevitos had forced Saddler to swallow had done the job it was concocted to do. It had wiped his memory clean. The only trouble was Saddler had no experiences and no memories to draw on to create the kind of powerful, deadly Creations that Crevitos required for his invincible army. Saddler had no imagination and just at this point, Crevitos felt as though he had come up against a brick wall. Currently, he could see no way around it.

There was a knock at the sturdy wooden door which guarded Crevitos's lofty retreat. Crevitos paused in his pacing just long enough to bark: "Enter," before resuming once more.

The head of his most trusted henchman appeared.

"Master."

"Ahh, Snake. I have a problem; a problem to which, at this moment, I can see no solution. Come. Sit."

Crevitos gestured towards the small bed which occupied one side of the curved room. Snake shifted the leather pouch which contained the long, sinuous tail from which he had gained his name, so that he could perch on the edge of the bed. It was just as well never to relax too much, or sit too comfortably, when Crevitos was around. He was liable to require instant action of some kind at any moment.

Snake waited silently while Crevitos sat on the only chair in the room.

"Saddler," began Crevitos.

Snake kept his face neutral. Saddler was a thorn in Snake's side, but he was Crevitos's pet project and, as such, it was wise not to comment on the subject. Snake had serious doubts about Saddler. He could not bring himself to believe that Saddler had lost his memory entirely, or that he had absolutely no idea who he was. To give voice to this thought, however, would be to criticize Crevitos. And to criticize Crevitos… Snake shuddered to think what the consequences of that would be. So, for now, he merely raised his eyebrows and listened intently to what his master had to say.

When Crevitos had finished explaining his problem, Snake thought quickly. Crevitos was not known for his patience, and he would want some kind of answer pronto. To buy a little time, Snake said; "So Saddler can't draw the right kind of Creations, because he has no imagination, right?"

Crevitos had begun to pace about the room again.

"Yes, yes, and you know how close we are to breaking through the gateway to Emajen. I need him to draw for me, now!"

While Crevitos was speaking, Snake flashed his almond-shaped eyes desperately around the room in search of some inspiration. His forked tongue flickered nervously across his lips. His gaze came to rest briefly on a pile of books on Crevitos's desk. Crevitos was a great reader, no doubt something he had absorbed from the young artist who had created him. No one on Doomland actually knew that Crevitos was a Creation (although Snake had his suspicions, why else would Crevitos be there?) but Crevitos believed passionately that knowledge was power, so he read anything and everything and, Creation or not, his knowledge and strength of character were forces to be reckoned with.

The book that Snake's eyes rested upon now appeared to show pictures of various kinds of creatures that he assumed came from another world outside of Doomland, and it was then that the idea struck him.

"So, if Saddler has no imagination…"

"Yes, Yes!" said Crevitos impatiently.

"Then, perhaps, you need to give him one."

Crevitos looked at Snake with an expression that suggested he might either explode with fury or be intrigued by the concept. To prevent the fury option from raising its ugly head, Snake continued hurriedly.

"What I mean is, maybe you need to feed his imagination. Take him somewhere, where there are lots of creatures that will build up a memory bank for his drawings."

There was a silence. Snake waited anxiously. His tongue flickered, in and out, in and out. Crevitos tilted his head slightly to one side as he considered Snake's suggestion. Then a cruel smile spread slowly across his beautiful face. Striding across the room (and much to Snake's tremendous relief) he slapped Snake heartily on the back.

"You are so right, Snake. I knew I could rely on you. And I know just where to take him. I shall take Saddler to Earth."

# CHAPTER THIRTEEN
# REVELATION

*The Prof had always loved inventing things, even when he had lived on his home world of Earth. Once on Emajen, however, his inventions had taken on a whole new level of creation due to the tremendous energies he encountered there. The two worlds weren't so very dissimilar in some ways, but Emajen's inhabitants had embraced its magical and mystical energies over the years, where most of Earth's people had left those things behind, preferring a more technological advancement. Not a great move in the Prof's opinion, and it was why he had decided to make his permanent home on Emajen!*

*Some of the Prof's inventions were - and he wasn't too proud to admit it - a bit of a disaster. Some, however, had proved extremely successful indeed. And he was particularly grateful that his healing ring had turned out to be one of the very best...*

Arrangements had been made. Although the initial trip to Earth would naturally be through a gateway, all other travelling would be done Earth style, to avoid arousing suspicion. Unless one were very careful, suddenly appearing and disappearing through a startlingly bright light and a large black inkblot (which were not normal Earth practices) might cause a little consternation.

Saddler himself, had been captivated by the way the bright light poured out of such a small box followed immediately by a rapidly expanding blob of darkness. Somewhere in his new consciousness, a feeling of familiarity stirred. However, he didn't have much time to think about this as Crevitos grabbed the collar of his jacket and thrust him into the blob. It was all very rapid. One minute they were on Emajen and the next they were on Earth.

Within that brief spell of time, some subconscious thought made Saddler thrust his hand into his pocket. He clutched the ring and traced its curves from head to tail in a now familiar movement. Whether it was the fact of going through the gateway, or just coincidence, Saddler would never know, but the familiar shock of energy that raced through him was by far the most powerful he had experienced yet. Without knowing how he knew, Saddler realized that the ring's power was now almost spent, and he would have to be very careful not to touch it again except in the greatest need.

As they stepped through the black blob, Saddler also knew something else: he was not who Crevitos wanted him to be. It felt as though there was now only the thinnest of gauze like veils across Saddler's mind. It wouldn't take too much, he thought, to lift it completely, and then he would know all the things he now knew he had forgotten. It was incredibly tempting to use the ring once more, except something about it didn't feel quite right. He would have to be patient for a while longer. Above all, Crevitos must suspect nothing.

Before they had arrived on Earth, it had occurred to Saddler to wonder what Earth inhabitants looked like and whether either Crevitos or he would be completely out of place. But Crevitos, who had an uncanny way of anticipating Saddler's thoughts, had shown Saddler some books of that world, and the beings called humans who lived there. Saddler had seen his own reflection in his window when the darkness, which was never far away, fell on Doomland, so he knew he was quite similar looking to some of Earth's human beings. About Crevitos, though, he was not so sure. Crevitos was very tall with a strikingly cruel, yet beautiful face. True, he appeared to have much the same body parts and features humans possessed, but Saddler had a sneaking feeling Crevitos would always stand out in any crowd, anywhere.

Such thoughts were temporarily pushed aside as they began their travels through a new world. Saddler had never been on a plane. (At least, he had on a previous visit to Earth, but not within his current memory.) He found it exciting and fascinating in equal measure. But not frightening, because he hadn't yet had any real reason to feel fear in his new existence. To be sure, he was wary of Crevitos (though Crevitos had been nothing but patient and kind up to this point) but he hadn't been anywhere apart from Crevitos's fortress, since he had taken the potion.

So now, they were on a plane heading to Puerto Maldonado from where they would travel by riverboat deep into the Amazon jungle. Their stay in the Manu Reserved Zone would be the first stage of Saddler's education about a variety of creatures; some with the deadly attributes Crevitos so desired Saddler to draw.

Once before, Saddler had asked the question: "Why can't you draw your own Creations?"

At the time, Crevitos had merely grunted something about not enough time, but now, in his new, heightened state of awareness, Saddler realized there must be something more to it. For the moment, though, he was bound by Crevitos's will. There was very little he could do, until the last pieces of the puzzle slotted into place, and he could finally see the whole picture.

For now, this seemed like a rather exciting adventure to be having, so Saddler decided to just sit back and enjoy the ride.

# CHAPTER FOURTEEN
# THE ADVENTURE BEGINS

*Looking back at his trip to Earth with Crevitos filled Saddler with very mixed feelings. On the one hand, the incredible things they had seen in the Amazon Rainforest were memories he would cherish forever. There were certain things about Earth, or at least the way Earth's people treated their world with such casual disdain, that he couldn't get his head around and honestly didn't much like, but there was no doubt that Earth itself was a stupendous world and some of its inhabitants, both flora and fauna, were truly fabulous. On the other hand, his memories of the visit were tainted with the horror of what he now knew to be the reason for their trip.*

*Everything came back to the fact that Saddler had been Crevitos's pawn. If things had gone differently, Saddler could easily have helped Crevitos to destroy Emajen and possibly even Earth too.*

*It didn't even bear thinking about…*

As the boat they were on glided smoothly along the Amazon River, Saddler gazed about him in awe. The vastness of the rainforest on either side, soaring up to the very top of the world it seemed, left him speechless. Crevitos himself was impressed and excited in a way that Saddler had never witnessed before. He knew by now that Crevitos loved to learn, and he was beginning to understand in some small way what made Crevitos tick. However, Saddler wasn't sure it was the incredible beauty and sheer majesty of the terrain that was the cause of Crevitos's enthusiasm.

As they journeyed, the river boat guide gave them a running commentary about the fantastic area surrounding them. The Amazon, he told them, is the world's largest tropical rainforest, with an area of around 5.5 million square kilometres. An area into which the United Kingdom and Ireland would fit seventeen times.

Neither the figure, nor the comparison meant anything to Saddler, but he guessed it must mean that it was unbelievably vast. Crevitos on the other hand seemed delighted and was keen for Saddler to share his enthusiasm.

"Imagine that, eh, Saddler. 5.5 million square kilometres. And this is only a small part of this entire world!"

Saddler smiled to show his appreciation, but his thoughts were dark: Yes, he was pretty sure that Crevitos's excitement was far more about future plans for multi-world domination (and what havoc could he wreak on a world such as this?) than about the incredible charm of the rainforest itself! Saddler sat silently with his thoughts until he was abruptly jolted out of them by a cry of sheer joy from Crevitos.

"Look!" he shouted. "There, Saddler, there!"

Saddler gazed in the direction of Crevitos's outstretched hand. A creature, such as none he had ever seen before (in his memory, anyway) ambled on four short, stout legs down the bank towards the river. It had a cruel, unhurried air about it that made Saddler shiver. Something about it made him think, that if it wanted to, it could suddenly move very swiftly indeed.

The guide, alerted by Crevitos's cry was busy telling them that this animal was called a Black Caiman, one of the alligator family. This particular species, the guide was saying, could grow to a length of more than nine feet and was heavily armoured with not only scales, but also interlocking bony plates beneath the scales themselves, making them virtually indestructible.

"You hear that?" Crevitos's eyes had lit up at this piece of information. "Virtually indestructible, Saddler!"

So here it was, the other reason for Crevitos's exuberance. Crevitos had not explained the reason for their journey to Saddler, but now the penny had dropped – Saddler would be expected to draw creations with features of these animals that would help Crevitos to create an army both deadly and invincible. Saddler could almost imagine Crevitos purring as the guide explained how ill-tempered and vicious Black Caimans are and how they are known to attack humans. He watched as the creature slid sinuously towards the water. It paused for a moment to yawn, displaying a cavernous jaw with rows of gleaming, razor sharp teeth. Then it slipped smoothly into the water and was gone.

For the rest of the journey to the lodge, where they would be based, Saddler tried incredibly hard to match Crevitos's joy at his discoveries. He could only hope, that in his own excitement, Crevitos did not notice that Saddler's reaction was rather less whole-hearted than his own.

# CHAPTER FIFTEEN
# DESPAIR

*Even for Nebiré, it had been a surreal experience following Saddler's journey through her visions. Her powers on other worlds were limited, and her visions were weakened also by the immense distance so, on many occasions, she couldn't hear what was being said. Often, though, Saddler's facial expressions and body language spoke volumes, and it soon became clear that Saddler had begun to distrust Crevitos, although Nebiré could only guess at the reason why.*

*She was just grateful that Crevitos was too absorbed in himself and his own designs to notice any changes in Saddler's behaviour...*

Their first guided tour through the Amazon Rainforest, was not scheduled until the following day. Crevitos, restless and impatient as always, decided to improve on his already impressive bank of knowledge by reading the guidebook from end to end.

Saddler was rather shaken by what he had seen, nonetheless, he felt compelled to try to sketch the menacing creature from the riverbank – the details were etched with total clarity in his mind: its long, thick powerful tail; its small, glinting eyes and that permanently evil grin, which housed a deadly bite.

As Crevitos read, he imparted various nuggets of information to Saddler in a voice deep with satisfaction.

"We certainly chose a good place to come, eh? This rainforest is about 55 million years old! You know what that means, Saddler? There will be creatures that have evolved and survived unbelievable hardships. They will be strong and powerful, with features, maybe, that we cannot yet begin to imagine."

Then he would pace for a few minutes before starting again.

"Oh, this is good. No, this is WONDERFUL! Would you believe, Saddler, that there are thought to be around 40,000 different varieties of plants – some especially mean ones, too. Then there are the birds, around 1,500 million of those. 2,000 species of fish, it says here and, unbelievably, 2.5 million species of insects. I imagine some of those are quite deadly."

The cruel smirk that was never far from Crevitos's lips, had surfaced readily at these facts.

"Ah, and here we have 430 different kinds of mammal. If even half of those are as impressive as that fellow we saw on the riverbank today, you will have enough ideas to last you a lifetime!"

When he received no response from Saddler, Crevitos finally glanced up. He had been so pleased with what he was learning, he hadn't really noticed whether Saddler was listening or not. Now he realised that Saddler was concentrating intently on something he was drawing. Striding across the floor, Crevitos stopped to look over Saddler's shoulder and his stern expression transformed into one of triumphant expectation. Saddler's recreation of the Black Caiman was so accurate that if the picture had moved on the page itself Crevitos would hardly have been surprised. He breathed in deeply and let out a long sigh of contentment. If Saddler could remember what he had seen this well, there would be no limit to the Creations he could draw, or the deadly features he could enhance them with.

"HA!" Crevitos slapped Saddler jovially on the back and strode back to his book, saying: "There are such discoveries to be made here, Saddler, and then, when we return to Doomland, there will be much work for you to do."

With his back turned, Crevitos did not see the look of fear and loathing etched on Saddler's face.

# CHAPTER SIXTEEN
# EXOTIC SURROUNDINGS

*It was a source of immense irritation to Crevitos that he couldn't, himself, adequately draw creations to build up his world-dominating army. Being a Creation himself meant that, formidable as he was in so many ways, the creations he drew were weak. It was a bit like making a tracing of a tracing - just not quite the same as the original.*

*Saddler, on the other hand, had proven himself to be very adept at drawing. Crevitos had high hopes that Saddler would create strong, fearsome creatures that could be crafted into a truly invincible fighting force.*

*Saddler's lack of imagination had been an unexpected stumbling block, but for once Snake had come up with a very passable solution…*

The next few days were a whirlwind of activity, with very little time for Saddler to brood upon the why's and the wherefores of his and Crevitos's visit here. Day one saw them leaving their lodge very early in the morning, ready to embark on an eight-hour journey across the Andes.

Exhausted from all the emotion and travelling of the previous day, Saddler alternately dozed on the tour bus or gazed fascinated from his window. Despite a couple of breaks in the journey, Saddler discovered that he was aching and stiff when he alighted from the bus. He soon forgot all about this however, as they began to trek their way through what he had learned was called the Cloud Forest. Having spent the only time in his life that he could remember either in Crevitos's room, or his own, this was almost too much for Saddler's brain to compute. Everywhere he turned, there was lush, green vegetation – so many different trees and plants, such a variety of colours and shapes, that he could barely take it all in.

Crevitos was listening intently to the guide, and Saddler tried hard to concentrate too, but his eyes were continuously drawn by the sight of pretty Skipper butterflies that darted here, there and everywhere, or by a pair of Capuchin monkeys high up in the branches of an enormous tree. This last sight held Saddler captivated for several minutes, as one monkey deftly groomed the other with its incredibly human-like hands. Their faces were amazingly human too: while one Capuchin concentrated hard on its grooming task, the other rested its chin on its hand with an expression of complete rapture. They seemed totally unfazed by the group chatting noisily below.

A few moments later, Saddler's thoughts were interrupted by a bellow from Crevitos. He looked up startled to find that the group was disappearing into a clump of trees, and he was in danger of being left behind in this teeming wilderness. Glancing up once more at the Capuchins, he was just in time to glimpse the very human-like fear on their faces as they scattered and disappeared into the branches.

He obviously wasn't the only one to be wary of Crevitos.

With a grim expression, Saddler hurried to catch up with the group.

When he reached them, everyone was standing at the base of a vast tree that soared high into the atmosphere. Here at ground level though, the roots snaked and tumbled over one another, disappearing off sinuously into the undergrowth. Saddler arrived just in time to hear the guide say that the tree was called Cola de Raton or, in English, Rat's Tail.

Rat's Tail is right, Saddler thought with a shudder, glad there weren't any real rats with tails that long. Just as this thought surfaced in his mind, he could feel Crevitos's gaze on him and knew immediately what Crevitos must be thinking. Carefully drawn, a Creation with a tail of that size would have a formidable weapon at its disposal. Saddler refused to be drawn by Crevitos's gaze, however, and pretended he was listening carefully to the guide.

Actually, what the guide was telling them was quite amazing, so just for a while Saddler was distracted from his thoughts of giant rats' tails. Apparently, this menacing looking tree was one of possibly around forty thousand species of plant that could be used to make medicines. This particular tree, he said, was very good for indigestion. Saddler wasn't sure what indigestion was, but decided he would look it up in the dictionary which had been one of Crevitos's recent strange gifts.

The reasoning behind this present was, he gathered, because Crevitos believed Saddler would need to be able to describe in his mind the Creations he would ultimately draw, using words as well as pictures. Now that Saddler knew what the purpose of his existence was, he didn't feel that he wanted to either describe or draw Creations. Having used the dictionary to find out what an invincible army was, every single atom of his being cried out against the thought of drawing creatures with the sole purpose of destroying others. There was so much in his brain that was hidden from him just now by the thinnest veil; he could sense all the knowledge just waiting to be set free. For now, he could only wait and hope that he would find out who he was before Crevitos made him do things he was really going to regret.

Already Saddler knew he had sketched Creations with guidance from Crevitos and these Creations were not strong enough, because they hadn't come from his own imagination. Nonetheless, they would still form part of this vast army that Crevitos was expanding daily, and Saddler felt sick that he'd had any part in it at all.

In no time at all, it seemed, their forest walk was over, so, exhausted from their long day of travel and discovery, the group retired to the rustic lodge in which they would spend the night.

Saddler's mind was reeling with everything he had seen and heard that day. They had (in Saddler's view) been extremely privileged to see some wondrous creatures during their walk, his favourite being the unbelievably beautiful Golden Headed

Quetzal with its brilliant trailing tail feathers, stunning plumage and aptly named head colouring. Crevitos, on the other hand, while he did not seem even remotely fatigued by their long day, was not so impressed.

"Hmph," he had growled testily. "I hope we are going to see some beasts with considerably more formidable features tomorrow. It is, after all, why we came here." He glowered at Saddler as though somehow the lack of ferocious animals they had seen on their walk was entirely Saddler's fault. Clearly expecting no answer, and subsequently receiving none from Saddler, Crevitos had stomped off to his sleeping quarters. Feeling extremely grateful to be on his own at last, Saddler found he could not rest until he had recorded both the Quetzal and the Capuchin monkey in his sketch book. Despite feeling shattered, it was some while before he lay down his pencil and gazed critically at his drawings. Finally, satisfied that he could do no more, Saddler threw himself onto his bed and fell at once into a deep dreamless sleep.

# CHAPTER SEVENTEEN
# MIXED FEELINGS

*As Anthony listened to Saddler's tale, he became more and more incredulous that one person could survive the traumas and horrors that Saddler had undoubtedly been through.*

*That Saddler would be scarred in some way was beyond doubt, but it was testament to his incredible strength of will and character that he could even begin to face retelling the events of his time in Crevitos's clutches. Anthony could see that Saddler was struggling with a huge amount of guilt. He knew Saddler blamed himself for the war on Emajen.*

*He was wrong of course - that had been entirely Crevitos's fault. Everything had been Crevitos's fault. How to help Saddler to understand that was another thing entirely. Anthony knew that the best thing they could do for him right now was just to listen.*

*And it was a remarkable tale, to be sure…*

The next day involved another early start and another bus journey to the tropical lowland forest. Tired, Saddler had mostly dozed until it had been time for them to transfer to a motorized canoe, in which they had navigated their way down the fast-flowing Alto Madre de Dios river. Finally, after about half an hour they had come across a lake where they had climbed aboard a traditional balsa raft to traverse the lake and take in the grandeur of the enormous rainforest.

Crevitos had been quiet throughout the day, and Saddler had found he was able to relax and absorb the wonderful surroundings in which he found himself. The forest buzzed with exotic wildlife: Muscovy ducks, Cormorants and Herons were plentiful and Squirrel monkeys chattered, played and swung among the tropical trees. The water too, was incredibly clear, and Saddler watched fascinated as a dazzling array of jewel-coloured tropical fish swam, glided and flitted about their business in their underwater world.

By late afternoon, Saddler thought his head might explode with all the exotic images swimming around in his brain. Fortunately, they soon arrived at the next lodge, right at the foot of a stunning mountain range, which towered majestically above them. Here they had a few hours to rest, before they were due to take an exploratory night walk through the forest.

Crevitos had disappeared to his lodgings without a word leaving Saddler to spend a happy couple of hours sketching the wonderful array of tropical creatures he had seen.

The next thing he knew, it was dark and Crevitos was roughly shaking his shoulder. Saddler rubbed his eyes and stared at Crevitos blearily for a moment or two before he remembered where he was.

"Is it time for our night walk?" he asked groggily.

"I told the guide we would not be going!" Crevitos said bluntly.

"Oh!" Saddler was confused.

"I told him we were fatigued and would resume with the tour in the morning. He quite understood. It's another early start after all."

Saddler didn't think he had ever seen anyone who looked less exhausted than Crevitos. In fact, it amazed him how much energy Crevitos radiated no matter how long or tiring the day had been.

He was just considering whether he felt more disappointed not to be going on the walk, or more relieved because, he was actually quite shattered, when Crevitos interrupted his thoughts with a single word.

"However…"

Saddler looked at Crevitos's face and knew that he wasn't going to like whatever Crevitos had to say next.

"… I have decided that we shall have an impromptu stroll of our own. There is far too much sticking to the tracks. I want to see the real, unscripted, unsentimental forest for myself. I want to see the creatures that hide in the places humans are wary to tread."

"But Crevitos…" spluttered Saddler, "it's a dangerous place – there are guides for a reason. Supposing one of us gets hurt, or… or bitten, or something?"

"PAH!" Crevitos was dismissive. "Nothing out there can hurt us. We are not from this world."

Saddler had his doubts. At least, he had doubts about his own safety – Crevitos, on the other hand, now he truly did seem indestructible. With a jolt of understanding, Saddler realized for the first time that he and Crevitos were very different. So different in fact… could it possible that Saddler himself was not from Doomland at all?

"Supposing we get lost? The rainforest is huge – they might never find us!"

"Saddler!" Crevitos's voice was condescending. He had busily been checking Saddler's rucksack, and he now produced a familiar object, which he waved significantly in Saddler's direction.

"You know as well as I do that we have only to step through the gateway and we can be back on Doomland in no time at all."

Saddler could think of nothing in answer to this. Glumly, he took the rucksack that Crevitos offered him, noting cynically that Crevitos himself was only carrying a torch. Then warily, he followed Crevitos out into the black, velvet night.

# CHAPTER EIGHTEEN
# THINGS THAT GO BUMP IN THE NIGHT

*Many Creations on Doodland (not Doomland as Crevitos had so malignly renamed it) including Boff himself, were certain that Crevitos was actually a Creation. Of course, they had no proof one way or the other, and, somehow, he possessed an unusual strength and energy that had allowed him to become incredibly powerful.*

*Boff, like so many other Creations, had spent more time than he cared to remember slaving in the mines of Doomland, bullied and cowed by Crevitos's henchmen. It was purely by chance that he had discovered a box - a very special box that, as it turned out, was a gateway between worlds. So, he had escaped from Doomland. But he, more than any of the others, understood just how impossible, not to say horrifying, Saddler's time must have been there…*

Saddler stumbled after Crevitos, wishing, with every step further into the forest, that he had thought to bring another torch for himself. It was quite likely, of course, that there was a torch in his rucksack, but Crevitos was striding off so quickly ahead of him, that there was simply no time to stop and check. Even during the daytime, the forest was eerie. At night, it was positively terrifying. There were rustles and noises and small lights that glinted briefly in the torchlight, only to flicker and disappear without trace. Crevitos pushed his way carelessly through the vegetation, thrusting aside the intertwining leaves and branches with no regard as to whether Saddler was managing to keep up or not.

Saddler lost all sense of time – the forest flowed around him like a dark, endless nightmare, filled with nameless terrors and untold hazards waiting for the opportunity to leap out and strike. Saddler was sweating with the exertion of keeping up with Crevitos; although it was partly due to fear – fear of losing sight of the torchlight that bounced and jolted with Crevitos's every step and fear of losing the shadowy figure of Crevitos himself, which moved swiftly and easily behind its beam.

Saddler's imagination was certainly working overtime now. If this had been Crevitos's intention, then it was definitely working. Feeling that his heart might actually give out at any moment, Saddler opened his mouth to call out to Crevitos. Two things happened almost instantaneously: Saddler caught his foot on a protruding tree root and, as he fell, something scuttled disgustingly across his sprawling hand and up his arm. It stopped short of his shirt sleeve, just above his elbow, and Saddler, now lying alone in the dark on the forest floor, could feel it quivering there.

How long he lay there it was impossible to tell, but it felt like a lifetime. Beneath him, the forest floor was a mass of gnarled roots and fallen twigs and branches. His discomfort grew with every passing moment, yet he dared not move or call out, so conscious was he of the presence that bristled and quivered on his upper arm. For the first time, Saddler thought that he might actually die here. He might spend the last few moments of his life on the hard, unforgiving floor of the Amazon rainforest, alone and not even knowing who he really was. Suddenly, it didn't seem to matter very much. His heart gradually stopped pounding and, in the pitch black of the world around him, he felt as though he would slowly sink into the forest floor to become part of this rich and diverse biosphere.

He didn't hear Crevitos return. One moment there was only darkness. The next, there was Crevitos, towering above him: the torchlight was blinding after the velvet blackness of the night. Saddler averted his eyes from the beam and his gaze was riveted by the large, hairy creature crouching menacingly on his arm. Two large eyes and six smaller ones glared at him belligerently, whilst eight strong, spiny legs rested lightly, as if ready to spring at the slightest provocation.

Saddler froze. The spider's red jaws trembled, for all the world as though it were mulling over just how tasty he might be. Red jaws. Red was bad, right? It meant danger – that's what he'd read. And this critter looked about as mean as you could get.

"What are you doing, Saddler?" Crevitos asked in an accusing tone. Even if he hadn't been paralyzed with fear, Saddler didn't believe there was really any answer for such a moronic question.

"For Doomland's sake, get up!" Crevitos extended a hand, but Saddler ignored it and flicked his eyes beseechingly at the horrifying creature residing on his arm.

"What?" At first Crevitos couldn't understand what Saddler was up to. Saddler flicked his gaze from Crevitos to his arm again.

"I don't … oh, what, you mean that little thing?"

Before he even had time to utter a sound of warning, Crevitos had swooped down and plucked the offending creature from Saddler's limb.

For a timeless moment, the spider and Crevitos locked eyes and stared hostilely at each other. The spider raised its front legs threateningly and readied itself to strike.

Crevitos laughed.

"Impressive set of fangs, little fellow. Another time, you and I might have a little fun."

Used to its victims trembling with fear, the spider finally quailed under Crevitos's dominant gaze. As quick as a flash it scrambled across the palm of his hand, dropped to the forest floor and disappeared into the dark night.

Saddler rose, shuddering, to his feet, aching all over from his fall and sticky with his own dried sweat. Crevitos had already turned, intent on making his way back into the rainforest.

"Wait!" Saddler called shakily, "I need a moment."

Crevitos tutted; nonetheless he stood, hands on hips, tall and imposing still, even in these majestic surroundings, waiting for Saddler to compose himself.

Saddler fumbled with his backpack, aware that Crevitos was not likely to give him long. To his immense relief, there, nestling amongst other various bits and pieces was a torch. He was even more relieved when he flicked the switch and a bright, illuminating light shone out before him. Quickly, he closed his backpack again and hung it over his shoulder, before straightening up to face Crevitos.

"Ready?" Crevitos raised a mocking eyebrow.

Saddler paused for just a moment, before nodding. In the rucksack, he had also glimpsed the box – the box that housed the gateway between worlds. For a split second, he had been tempted (actually, very tempted) to open the box and disappear back to Doomland, leaving Crevitos stranded in the rainforest. Two further thoughts though, had immediately squashed the first. The box needed a key, which in that brief moment he hadn't seen. And Crevitos was supernaturally quick. The likelihood that Saddler could find the key, unlock the box and utter the name of a place to disappear to, before Crevitos closed the short gap between them, was highly improbable. And then of course, the game would be up. Crevitos would know that Saddler was more aware of his situation than he should be.

The second thought, equally sobering, was that the only other place Saddler knew about was Doomland. He was pretty sure now, that Doomland was not his original world, however that was as far as his understanding went.

Until – or indeed if – his full memory ever returned, there was no point in even trying to escape Crevitos. Being alone and friendless on Doomland would be no help at all.

Now, standing in the middle of the Amazon rainforest, in the dead of night, staring at Crevitos's ruthless yet stunning face by torchlight, Saddler knew he had to continue to play the game for a while longer.

"Good," Crevitos was saying. "Come, I have something most interesting to show you."

As Crevitos turned to go, something silver, hanging on a chain around his neck, glinted in the light of Saddler's torch. The key! Saddler smiled humourlessly to himself. Of course Crevitos had the key. Crevitos trusted no one, even someone he believed had no mind of his own. Dispirited, Saddler took a deep breath and strode after him.

They actually didn't have far to go, before Crevitos abruptly came to a halt. Unaware of Crevitos's intention to stop, Saddler almost collided with him, nearly letting the torch slip from his hand.

As always, Crevitos paid little attention to anyone's requirements but his own.

"Yes! This is the spot!" he said gleefully.

Saddler looked at Crevitos astounded. They were in the heart of the Amazon rainforest. It was pitch black. As far as he, Saddler, could see in the limited circumference of his torchlight, it all looked the damn same. How on Emajen did Crevitos know that this was the spot.

"Ah! Come to me, my little beauty." Crevitos was bending to retrieve something and obviously expected Saddler's full attention. But Saddler was distracted. Emajen. Where had that come from? It was so familiar, but what did it mean?

"Well?" A hint of impatience in Crevitos's tone wrenched Saddler sharply back into focus. The puzzle of Emajen would have to wait.

Crevitos was tall, but even so the creature he was holding trailed along the ground for almost half its length again, even though Crevitos was holding it up at head height.

"Now, this," crowed Crevitos, "Is more like it, Saddler. Meet the Bushmaster Pit Viper."

Saddler looked from the expression of savage joy on Crevitos's face to the triangular shaped head of the snake he was holding. In the eerie light from his torch, it looked as though the viper must be at least ten feet long, with black or brown diamond shaped markings all down its back that expanded and contracted as it wriggled helplessly in Crevitos's grasp.

"Impressive, eh?" Crevitos laughed. "And it has quite a fearsome bite on it too." Crevitos held up his free hand to show

Saddler two deep puncture wounds where he had been bitten by the Bushmaster's extremely long fangs.

Saddler watched carefully. Crevitos seemed totally unaffected by his injury; indeed, he was delighted with his success in finding such a fine specimen.

"Well, Saddler, take a really good look. I want you to imprint every feature of this beauty on to your brain, as I trust you have done with our little spider friend!"

Crevitos held the snake aloft for a few moments more, to ensure that Saddler was taking a good look. Then, with an expression almost of regret, he lay it quite gently back on the ground, where he had found it.

Saddler watched the scene unfold, mesmerized. He shone his torch on the viper as Crevitos let go, to reassure himself that it didn't make a beeline for him. As he watched, Saddler could swear the snake looked at Crevitos with fear in its eyes, before it slithered with deadly silence off into the undergrowth.

Crevitos slapped Saddler on the back as he passed, saying: "A good night's work, I think." Then he strode off back the way he had come, as if they were on a pleasant afternoon stroll.

# CHAPTER NINETEEN
# EXPLANATIONS

*Despite being a great big bear of a man, the Prof had always been a gentle giant. His kind nature was one of the reasons that he had elected to live on Emajen rather than on Earth.*

*Until Crevitos began to attack the very fabric of Emajen's existence, the Prof had never heard of a battle happening there. Life wasn't perfect on Emajen, any more than it was anywhere else, but the Natorqua seemed able to keep Emajen and its inhabitants on an even keel.*

*Listening to Saddler's story had, in truth, made the Prof feel a little guilty. He had done his part to save Emajen, it was true, but he had also more-or-less abandoned his own world, which definitely had its own share of troubles. Perhaps he would have to pay the Amazon Rain Forest a visit in due course, but for now, he was fascinated by the tale that Saddler had to tell…*

Gathered together in Nebiré's house once more, the group were listening spell bound to Saddler's account. Destiny had shuddered, horrified at Saddler's re-telling of the spider incident. Much as she loved animals, spiders were most certainly not her favourites. She never deliberately hurt them (after all, they had a right to live their lives too) but sometimes, it took some courage to put a cup over the top of the bigger ones and a piece of paper underneath, then transport them outside to let them go.

The thought of one the size of your hand actually sitting on you…

"Did you find out what kind of spider it was?" Squib asked shyly, always keen for information on any topic.

"Oh yeah," answered Saddler. "It was a long walk back to the lodge that night, I can tell yer, or at least it seemed like it. There was no sign of anyone else, they was all back and fast asleep after their walk. But was we allowed to rest? Oh, no. Crevitos insisted we look up what we'd found and then I 'ad to sketch 'em before 'e'd let up."

Saddler paused for breath, shaking his head at the memory. Then he continued.

"Brazilian Wandering Spider. That's what it was. According to the book, it's called that 'cos it wanders about the jungle floor waitin' for fings it can attack. Oh, yeh, venomous too - vicious fings."

"Oh my gosh, Saddler, you must have been terrified!" Destiny was aghast.

"Well, it wasn't very nice, that's for sure."

"What about the Bushmaster?" Anthony asked. "What did you find out about that?"

"Well, 'ere's the fing, apparently, they're pretty aggressive and their name means 'silent death', on account of they use their colouring as camouflage and hide on the forest floor, waiting for their prey.

"But they're not poisonous though? You said Crevitos was bitten," said Boff.

"Venomous, my dear chap," exclaimed the Prof. "Poison is something you drink, venom is injected. A snake's fangs act a bit like a hypodermic needle, and they can inject venom very deeply and effectively."

"And yeah," continued Saddler, "Bushmaster vipers are venomous. In fact, it's the deadliest snake in the rainforest." Saddler straightened his shoulders and set his gaze into the distance, as though he were a schoolboy about to recite his lines.

"Bushmaster venom affects the circulatory system," he said. "It destroys the red blood cells, causing organ degeneration and massive tissue damage. Its primary function is to immobilize its prey, and the venom causes vomiting, severe pain, nausea, chills and eventually death."

"Whoa!" Anthony shook his head in admiration. "How can you remember all that after all you've been through?"

Saddler smiled rather sheepishly. "I fink that potion had a lasting effect on me brain. Seems like I'm a walking encyclopaedia these days!"

"Think I could do with some of that for my exams!" laughed Destiny.

"So, it's hugely pois… I mean venomous," Boff said slowly. "And yet Crevitos was bitten by it. Why didn't he die?"

"That's a good question," Saddler said darkly. "All the way back through the forest, 'e was chattering on like we'd just been for a jolly picnic. Never showed no signs 'e'd been bitten – not one! That's when I first realized 'e couldn't be 'uman, like."

"So, what about the rest of your visit? Did anything like that happen again?" asked Destiny.

"Nah. The last couple of days was quite uneventful, and I was glad about that, I can tell you. We did see some more pretty fantastic animals, but from a safe distance you might say."

Smiling at Nebiré, Saddler then said: "But there was one strange thing that 'appened right at the end. At least I thought it was strange at the time, cos it took us several thousand miles to our next destination, and I couldn't quite understand what made Crevitos want to go there.

# CHAPTER TWENTY
# ANOTHER CONUNDRUM

*It had never ceased to amaze both Anthony and Destiny that when they met Saddler for the very first time, it was actually for the second time.*

*When Saddler had initially approached them - well, accosted might be a more appropriate word - at the horse show in London, Anthony had been certain that he knew this strange person from somewhere, but he simply couldn't remember where or when that might have been. It was very much later, when Saddler had explained to them about the trouble Emajen was in and how he had gone to Earth seek help, that they realised where they had seen him before. It had been on the ranch in America, owned by Anthony's dad. Saddler had been there - and in a very garish shirt…*

It was the last day of their tour and Crevitos was happy. They had achieved what they had set out to achieve – Saddler had a whole sketchbook of creatures big and small. Most had one thing in common – a deadly feature that could be used as weapons for the greatest fighting force the universe had ever seen.

Secretly, Saddler had kept a small notebook of creatures he had seen that were exotic and beautiful, yet not necessarily with that deadly twist. However, there was one animal that both he and

Crevitos agreed on as being truly magnificent (though not for the same reason).

They had been travelling by boat down the Manu river. Saddler was more than happy: the boating trips gave Crevitos far less opportunity to take it into his head to go on another impromptu trek of his own. They had glimpsed a number of animals on the river shore: a couple more Black Caimans; a giant bushy tailed anteater and even a sleepy, hairy sloth hanging upside-down from the branch of a tree.

At this point, Saddler had sensed that Crevitos was getting restless. Whilst Saddler was enthralled with all the amazing sights and sounds of this most incredible journey, Crevitos was only interested in one thing, deadly animals. Then Crevitos had clutched Saddler's arm.

"There, Saddler – look! Is that not magnificent?"

And there, as cool and suave as you like, was a Jaguar sauntering lithely out of the forest. Ignoring all the busy life going on around it, the Jaguar stopped to inspect one huge, powerful paw, which it licked unhurriedly before replacing it confidently on the ground. Then it yawned a wide, leisurely yawn revealing such impressive canines that Saddler thought Crevitos would surely choke.

"See that? See that?" Crevitos could barely contain his excitement.

Even the guide was enthusiastic. Jaguars were a rare sight to see, being solitary creatures and generally very shy. He explained that the name Jaguar comes from the native American word Yaguar, meaning, 'he who kills with one leap'. One powerful bite from that truly awesome set of teeth would, apparently, herald the end of the toughest prey. Saddler could well believe it!

This Jaguar seemed anything but wary as it made its way down to the river, its distinctive rose like markings rippling sinuously with every footfall. Although it took no notice of its surroundings, yet it seemed to Saddler as though the Jaguar knew perfectly well they were there. The slow, relaxed movements demonstrating the obvious strength behind those powerful muscles seemed like a deliberate pose to Saddler. 'I'm boss', it appeared to say with every languid movement, 'Don't mess with me!' Saddler glanced at Crevitos and couldn't restrain himself from saying: "For some reason it reminds me of you!"

Crevitos stretched his mouth wide in a remarkably Jaguar-like grin, although his gaze remained fixed on the splendid beast before them.

Saddler realized he couldn't have said anything more likely to please Crevitos if he'd tried: praising Crevitos certainly hadn't been his intention.

Now they were waiting for the bus to take them back to Cusco where they had begun their trip. Although it had been a fabulous excursion, Saddler was not sorry it was coming to an end. In his room back on Doomland, Crevitos had spent time with Saddler for sure, but there had also been many hours when Saddler had been on his own. Being with Crevitos day in and day out, trying to keep up with his relentless energy, was, Saddler decided, exhausting.

He shuddered to think what he would have to do when they arrived back on Doomland, yet being back in his quiet fortress room once more would be quite a relief.

As they sat on the bus, Crevitos – restless as always – flicked idly through some leaflets he had picked up from one of the lodges. Mostly they were about other tropical rainforest trips and excursions, but one very different leaflet caught his eye.

He considered it carefully for a while, before saying to Saddler: "I think we shall make a small detour on the way home. I've a mind to see what can be learned here."

He handed the leaflet to Saddler whose heart had sunk at this proposal. It was advertising a holiday ranch over 4,000 miles northwest of their current position. According to the leaflet, it was not only a chance to experience some stunning scenery from horse-back, but also a unique opportunity to learn, from a top horse whisperer, how horses view the world.

Hardly a small detour and Saddler doubted very much that Crevitos would find anything very dangerous or formidable there.

He looked closely at the leaflet once more, trying to fathom what Crevitos's motive could be for visiting this place. The more he looked, the more he had a strange feeling that he'd seen this ranch before. Not just seen it but been there.

Yes, he was sure he'd been there. Saddler felt a sudden lifting of his spirits. Perhaps on this ranch he would finally find out who he really was.

# CHAPTER TWENTY-ONE
# LIGHTNING STRIKES

*Natorqua - definition: a stunning, hybrid, cat-horse creature, with - as yet little understood - mystical powers. Known to be the source of the peaceful ecological equilibrium on its native world (again, very little research has been undertaken into this phenomenon).*

*Temperament: Placid, affectionate and easily approachable.*

*Place of Origin: Emajen*

*Natural state: Living within a herd, protected overall by the Alpha Female.*

*Natural Enemies: No known foes or predators within the world of Emajen itself.*

**Post BoE (Battle of Emajen) update: The very essence of Emajen itself was put at considerable risk, due to the psychological attack on the Natorqua by one malevolent Crevitos, resident and ruler of otherworld Doomland (previous name Doodland - recently reverted to this title) …*

At some point on the long, involved journey from the Amazon rainforest to Wyoming where they would visit the ranch, Saddler had asked Crevitos what a horse whisperer was and why he was so keen to meet this one.

Crevitos had been evasive. He had merely said that horse whisperers don't whisper, they learn about how a horse thinks and feels. That was pretty much all Saddler could get out of him.

Saddler knew that Crevitos wanted to create a super fighting force and that in some way, he Saddler, needed to draw creatures with powerful and deadly features to help Crevitos do that. What he didn't know, was why. Who was Crevitos going to fight?

Of course, Saddler also knew now that there were more worlds than just Doomland, because he was on one right now. He also knew you could get to other worlds by going through the gateway in the box – but could you get a whole army through that way? And was it here, on Earth, that Crevitos wanted to bring his army? And, again, why? What had the people on Earth ever done to Crevitos? Plus, how had finding out how horses think have anything at all to do with creating an army?

There were so many questions spinning around in Saddler's head, he thought he might very well go completely crazy. Asking Crevitos for answers, was, of course, out of the question. If he wanted Saddler to know about his plans, he would tell him: and Saddler had a strong feeling that he shouldn't really have these questions in his mind at all!

The word Emajen suddenly flitted across his thoughts again, as though it were trying to catch his attention. Emajen was a place – somehow, he knew it. Was it on Earth, or was it another world?

Bits and pieces were beginning to fit together in Saddler's brain, like tiny fragments of a huge jigsaw. He felt frustratingly close to knowing what he didn't know, but what he felt he should know. As they finally arrived, at the end of their journey, Saddler looked around him, confused.

Grey Ranch – he'd definitely been here before, he knew he had, but when? How? Feeling dazed, he followed Crevitos who was striding off with his usual boundless energy towards their cabin. He was deep in conversation with a ranch hand and, for the moment, almost seemed to have forgotten Saddler.

As Saddler hurried to catch Crevitos up, an horrendous noise rent the air. Jolted out of his daze, he spun around to see where it was coming from.

Two men were desperately trying to calm a dog, which seemed to have become entangled in some fence wire. Suddenly, around the corner flew a young girl. Saddler watched mesmerised. He was too far away to hear what was being said, but the girl seemed to be instructing the men what to do.

He watched, fascinated, for quite some time as the girl very slowly, very carefully approached the dog. He could sense the connection she was creating between her and the animal. The ranch was so still, you could hear a pin drop and a kind of electricity crackled in the air.

Saddler jumped, startled, as a hand landed unceremoniously on his shoulder.

"There you are. Do come on, Saddler." Crevitos was, as usual, impatient. In his world there was always something important to do – never any time to waste. He was totally oblivious to what was happening by the fence and began to stride off in the direction of the cabin again, clearly expecting Saddler to follow.

Saddler duly obeyed, but something made him turn back. As he did so, the girl looked up from the dog, which was now buried in her arms. She smiled at the two men standing with her and, in that very moment, Saddler reeled as though he had been struck by a fierce flash of lightning.

Destiny. The girl's name was Destiny.

Like a dam bursting its barrier, Saddler's life gushed and poured overwhelmingly through his synapses, filling every gap, every nook and cranny that had been starved of understanding and memories ever since he had swallowed that damned potion. Stumbling blindly behind Crevitos, Saddler's chest heaved with emotion. Now he understood! Now everything made sense!

Now, finally, Saddler knew who he was!

# CHAPTER TWENTY-TWO
# COMPLICATED STRATEGIES

*Playing with time, reflected Nebiré, had definitely been of key importance in the tremendously challenging attempt to save both Emajen and Saddler.*

*She had known at the time what a huge risk she was taking. Tampering with the fabric of time on your own world was perilous enough and was never to be undertaken lightly: playing with time on another world, well now, that was a different matter entirely. There were so many permutations to consider, so many possible pitfalls to contemplate. She had very quickly realised, however, that there was nothing else to be done.*

*Somehow, the strands that had brought Anthony and Destiny to Emajen, and Saddler to his current state, needed to be woven together. It was the only way she could see that she could give Saddler a chance - and it was a slim one at that...*

"Woah there." Anthony leapt to his feet, a look of incredulous disbelief on his face. "How, Saddler? How?"

Everyone was looking at Saddler and each other and back at Saddler again, with total confusion.

"This makes no sense at all!" Anthony exclaimed.

Destiny, however, was calm. She touched Anthony's arm lightly. Shaking his head with puzzlement, he slowly sat down again.

"That's when you first saw us, wasn't it Saddler? It was the day mum and I arrived at the ranch too. Harriet had caught her paw in some wire just after we got there."

"But," interrupted Anthony, "That was way before we had even met each other, let alone Saddler. We didn't know anything about Emajen then. So how could Saddler be visiting the ranch AFTER he'd disappeared when we on our way to find the Natorqua?"

Destiny smiled, "I think perhaps Nebiré might have to tell us the next part of the story!"

Nebiré returned Destiny's smile and began to explain in her sonorous voice.

"If you recall," she began slowly, "I lost sight of Saddler once he had swallowed the potion. But the Prof had told me about the ring he'd made you, and I knew its properties were strong."

Here she inclined her head towards the Prof as a mark of her respect for him. He nodded in return, and she continued her explanation.

"In a vision, I saw you give the ring to Saddler. I could only hope that in some way it would work for him in his time of greatest need. So, I kept my eye on Saddler over the coming days. Every so often, there were flashes of insight and soon I realized that he must be gaining some strength from the ring.

"One of the strongest of those insights was when you first wrote your name, Saddler. That gave me hope; it seemed that there was some chance you might regain your memory after all."

"So," Anthony interrupted, "You knew, through a vision, when Crevitos was going to take Saddler to Earth, then."

"Indeed, and it gave me an opportunity to help."

Here, Saddler flashed Nebiré a look of gratitude. "You'll never know 'ow grateful I am. I don't know if I would ever 'ave found a way to escape Crevitos wivout your 'elp."

"There is no need for gratitude," Nebiré said solemnly. "Every single one of us here played a part in ridding Emajen of Crevitos's tyranny."

"And Doodland!" Boff remarked cheerily.

"It would appear so, yes."

"You mean Crevitos isn't on Doom… I mean Doodland, anymore?" Anthony asked astonished.

"Apparently," said Boff eagerly, "there was quite a reception waiting for him when he escaped back through the gateway." His lightbulbs darkened for a moment, before he continued. "They couldn't catch him, more's the pity, but he hasn't been seen on Doodland since. You wouldn't believe how different it is now."

"I must visit," said Saddler, "It was a barren wasteland when I was there last!"

"So," said the Prof, bringing the conversation back to Nebiré's story. "You knew Saddler would be going to Earth, but that still doesn't explain how Saddler and Crevitos arrived at the ranch when they did."

Suddenly a small voice piped up from beside the Prof. "Can I tell, please, Nebiré?" Squib looked at her with expectant hope shining on his young face. She returned his look with a radiant smile of agreement.

"Well," began Squib hesitantly, "Nebiré couldn't let Saddler and Crevitos visit Earth in the present, because, Destiny, you gave your granddad the potion to freeze time on Earth while you were looking for the Natorqua."

"Of course," said Destiny excitedly, "Crevitos would have known something was up then, for sure!"

"Yes," continued Squib, "So Nebiré needed to make them visit Earth in the past. Is that right?"

"You are entirely correct young Sebastian, Quentin, Isaiah, Brown," agreed Nebiré.

"Gosh, that must have been a pretty tall order," said Anthony.

"Not for Nebiré!" It was the first time Kaz had spoken. Destiny rubbed him lovingly on the nose.

"It involved much too-ing and fro-ing between here and Doomland (as it was then). It required finding someone close enough to Crevitos who could be trusted to place a small amount of substance in Crevitos's gateway box, just before he and Saddler were about to leave. Fortunately, Master Sebastian,

Quentin, Isaiah, Brown here was a most able, not to say courageous messenger."

"But I thought you and the Prof were on your way to find us. This is so confusing," said Boff.

"It was necessary for him to visit Doomland a few times along the way," Nebiré said by way of explanation.

"And you knew what to do, how exactly?" Destiny asked Squib.

"Birds carrying messages!" Anthony chipped in.

"Silly of me. Of course!"

"Needless to say," the Prof said amused, "Nebiré had it all in hand."

Boff heaved a huge sigh: "So," he said, "You and Crevitos visited Earth in the past, Saddler. That at least makes sense now."

"But," Anthony took up the thread, "Why on Earth would there be a leaflet about Grey Ranch in a lodge in the middle of the Amazon Rainforest over four thousand miles away…" He stopped abruptly, "Oh, OK, I get it. That was a set-up too. I was going to say, I didn't think Dad would have advertised quite that far away!"

They all knew that Nebiré had certain mystical powers, but it was beginning to dawn on Anthony just how incredible she really was.

"So, basically, you engineered it all so that Saddler and Crevitos came to the ranch just as Destiny and I were there at the same time. But what was your plan when they got there then?"

"Ah!" Saddler looked at Nebiré, who nodded, so he took up the telling of the story once more.

"As you know, I was pretty shocked by all the memories that came flooding back when I saw you, Destiny. And now I 'ad another problem. Some'ow I 'ad to pretend as if nothing 'ad 'appened. I daren't let slip what I knew, otherwise it would be curtains for me, before I could even begin to think of escaping, or trying to 'elp Emajen!" Saddler's voice wobbled. Kaz wandered slowly across to him and rested his head on Saddler's shoulder. After a moment or two, Saddler took a deep breath and continued more steadily again.

"For a while there, I was at me wits end. I didn't know what to do and it felt like time was running out fast." He paused. "Then I received a rather strange visitor."

# CHAPTER TWENTY-THREE
# A SHOCKING TURN OF EVENTS

*Everyone living on Emajen knows that the Natorqua are essentially their world's lifeblood, although no one has really ever questioned why, or how; they have always just taken it for granted.*

*Crevitos, in his efforts to undermine and eventually conquer Emajen, soon discovered this fact and realised that he could use it to his advantage. It didn't take him very long to work out how to infect the minds of the herd with poisonous thoughts that gradually turned them from being strong, yet gentle and placid into viciously disturbed creatures. The very fabric of their existence being so badly disrupted caused them to slowly fail and die, which suited his purposes excellently.*

*There were two downsides, however. One, was the length of time it was taking for the herd to die and two, was the fact that he hadn't yet succeeded in finishing off the Alpha Female. All the while she resisted him, the herd would - albeit depleted - survive. There was something more he needed to learn, and he just happened to have found a place where he might find out what that elusive thing was…*

For a couple of days, Crevitos seemed to be fully engaged in quizzing the people at the ranch and trying to find out as much about horse psychology as possible. Saddler was left to his own devices, which suited him well, as it meant he didn't have to keep up the pretence with Crevitos that nothing had changed.

His mind was a whirl of confusion: he felt trapped with no obvious sign of how he might escape from Crevitos's clutches. Now that his memory had returned, there were things, too, that he was aware of that filled him with dread; things that he couldn't fully bring himself to think about.

For that couple of days, being on Grey's Ranch was a soothing balm to his troubled soul. He spent a lot of time with the horses, which he loved (nators, he recalled they were on Emajen) and he made friends with Harriet the dog, who seemed to know in some way that he was troubled: she would often quietly sit with her head reassuringly on his knee.

As he wandered around the ranch, he watched the other guests going out for treks on the horses and thought that maybe it would be an enjoyable thing to do. He decided to find someone to ask, so he began to make his way back to the house. On the way he noticed a group of people standing by the fence of one of the corals. They were watching a young girl having a riding lesson; to his amazement, he realized that she had a blindfold on. As he watched from a slight distance, he heard music playing and could see that the horse was moving in time to it.

Beyond the far fence, other people were being drawn by the spectacle, but just at that moment, the music slowed and stopped. The girl whipped off the blindfold and it gave him a jolt when he realized it was Destiny. This whole situation was something he was having a job to get his head around, although he suspected that Nebiré must be involved in some way. Nonetheless, it was all very unnerving.

Shaking his head to try to clear his thoughts, Saddler glanced across at the small group of people who had arrived on the other side of the coral. One, a strikingly beautiful lady with tremendously long, golden hair stood out from the rest. There was something familiar about her, and Saddler felt momentarily taken aback. As Destiny walked her horse towards the gate, the group on the far side shifted.

Saddler's heart leapt into his mouth.

Time stopped.

Saddler was rooted, frozen to the spot.

He watched, transfixed, as the golden-haired lady now chatted amiably to… HIM!

There, in the brightest patterned shirt Saddler had ever seen, was someone who looked exactly like him.

Not just looked like.

It was.

Saddler was looking at himself.

The lady glanced up and caught his eye. She smiled, and even at such a distance, Saddler caught the brief wink that set his heart pounding once again. Don't worry, the wink told him, I'm here to help you. Baffled, Saddler turned and staggered away. What on Emajen was going on? He needed to find a way to talk to the woman with the golden hair, that much he did know. Another thing that struck him with absolutely clarity was that he must never be seen by the other Saddler. He couldn't have said why this was so important – but it was a very strong feeling.

Until such time as he could talk to the lady with the golden hair, Saddler thought it best to keep a low profile. That in itself was a big ask with Crevitos around – he had a way of attracting attention whether he wanted to or not.

Then another thought crossed Saddler's mind. Supposing Crevitos saw the bright-shirted Saddler – or even thought it was him? It was all too much to even think about. Somehow this lady was involved and somehow Nebiré was involved, and Saddler could only hope that there were forces at work which could keep Crevitos and Saddler's other self apart.

Saddler squared his shoulders. He had to stay strong; he had to find a way back to Emajen and he had to find a way of defeating Crevitos.

Maybe going for that trek was a good place to start. It would give him some breathing space to try to get his head around everything. Maybe horses on this world couldn't talk, but they still had the amazing ability to calm your spirit and give you strength to deal with what lay ahead.

Feeling more cheerful already, Saddler strode purposefully towards the house once more.

# CHAPTER TWENTY-FOUR
# A RAY OF HOPE

*There was no question that Saddler's time with Crevitos had been an horrendous one. And yet, there had been moments - things like the awe and wonder he had felt as they travelled through the rainforest - when he had been almost happy.*

*The revelation, on Grey's Ranch, of who he was and how dire the situation was had certainly changed all that. Nonetheless, Crevitos had continued to believe that Saddler was still his pawn, his plaything - his slave. How Saddler had continued to perpetuate that little piece of deception, he would never know.*

*Sometimes the horror and guilt that Saddler's memories evoked would have been overwhelming, if it hadn't been for his most wonderful friends…*

Mr Grey himself was manning the reception when Saddler walked in. From all the years he had spent with horses and people, he was quick to perceive what kind of mood either man or beast might be in. He could tell, despite Saddler's outwardly cheery demeanour, that his guest was feeling troubled.

Of course, he told Saddler, it would be no problem at all to arrange a ride out for him. In the interests of safety though, here at Grey's Ranch, they would ask that Saddler have a short riding lesson with one of their very experienced ranch hands just to be sure what kind of rider he was.

"That makes sense." Saddler could see entirely why it would be less than ideal to let just anyone ride off on one of your horses without knowing if they could ride. On Emajen, Saddler thought wistfully, you could ask a nator for a carry and they were almost always willing to oblige. There was no need for things like saddles or bits of metal in their mouths, you could just mount up and say where you wanted to go.

He realized now that there were many reasons why horses on Earth might be spooky or unpredictable, but nators on Emajen were usually very laid back; they didn't have a great deal to worry about.

Mind you, things had changed somewhat since Crevitos had been on the scene. Realizing that Mr Gray had said something and seemed to be waiting for an answer, Saddler dragged his thoughts back to the present.

"I'm sorry, I missed that," he said apologetically.

"I was just saying that we have another guest about to have a session in around ten minutes. You'd be welcome to join in."

Saddler hesitated just for a moment; supposing the other guest was the other him? He cast his mind back to when he had last visited Gray's Ranch, long before he had met Destiny and Anthony and long before the whole quest for the Natorqua had begun. He had ridden there certainly, but he most definitely hadn't had a lesson with himself – not that he could remember. But was this the past, or did time here on Earth play out in some kind of continuous loop with the same things happening over and over again? Oh well, things undoubtedly couldn't get any more bizarre. He would just have to hope for the best.

"Yeah, that would be great," he said. "Fanks"

***

The other guest, it transpired, was none other than the golden-haired lady Saddler had seen by the coral. By the time he arrived at the meeting place, she was already mounted and chatting to one of the tallest people Saddler had ever seen – taller than Crevitos even, he guessed.

This, it turned out, was Merlin the ranch hand. He was also the horse whisperer Crevitos had been so keen to meet. He was surrounded by a powerful aura of calm which seemed to radiate off him like warm rays of relaxing sunshine. Unhurriedly, he touched the horse lightly on its neck before loping in great languid strides across the yard towards Saddler.

Saddler's hand was immediately engulfed in a firm, welcoming handshake, and he found himself relaxing for the first time since he had come to Earth.

Merlin fetched the horse that Saddler was to ride. As it wasn't a riding lesson as such, the horse was tacked up and ready to go. Saddler lay his hand on the horse's neck lightly as he had just seen Merlin do. The horse turned its head slightly towards him and sighed. Although Saddler knew that Earth horses couldn't communicate like nators, nonetheless it felt quite natural to him to say:

"Alright fella? Do you fink I might be so bold as to ask for a carry?"

The horse's ears flicked at his voice and planted themselves firmly forwards. Merlin, who always watched closely when he first introduced one of his precious charges to a guest, nodded appreciatively. He was just about to indicate the mounting block – much better for a horse's back than mounting from the ground – when Saddler, with unexpected spring, leapt lightly onto the saddle. Despite the fact that Saddler was obviously no youngster, he had clearly been doing this for many a year.

Merlin was delighted. He had already realized that the other guest was a very competent horse person – and, much more pleasingly, had obvious empathy with her horse. Now it seemed that Saddler was very much cut from the same cloth.

It was a brief session. Merlin watched the pair walk, trot and canter keeping a close eye on the way they executed transitions between the different gaits. He didn't approve of kicking to make a horse move. As he always said, if someone kicked him, it certainly wouldn't make him want to do as he was told. He also watched how they came back down from a faster pace to a slower one and then to halt. Pulling at the reins to slow the horse down was not something he approved of either, although it was something too many riders did.

Both his guests had rather different riding styles, though effective in their own ways. Saddler talked to his horse a great deal, asking politely for changes of direction and pace. He sat lightly in the saddle and gave virtually no aids that Merlin could detect other than through his voice. The horse strangely seemed to understand exactly what Saddler was asking and appeared very happy to oblige.

The young lady on the other hand said nothing. Again, although she sat lightly astride her horse, she held the reins only gently in one hand and almost seemed to send her directions through telepathy as far as Merlin could tell.

He had never seen anything like it and made a mental note to have a chat with these two before they left the ranch.

He needed merely a few minutes to assess that these guests would be more than capable of riding out without an escort. It was ranch policy that guests were not allowed to ride out alone, for obvious reasons, so he enquired if they would be happy to go for a trail ride together.

Saddler glanced at the lady, who smiled warmly back. Again, that strange feeling that he knew her swept over him.

"Yeah, I fink that would do very nicely indeed."

With a few instructions from Merlin and a map of possible trails to hand, Saddler and his new acquaintance were soon on their way.

# CHAPTER TWENTY-FIVE
# AN IDENTITY REVEALED

*If you were able to alter your appearance to anything you wanted it to be, would you? To Saddler, indeed to everyone on Emajen, Nebiré was incredibly beautiful in her own guise.*

*On Emajen, people, beings - any sentient being - was accepted for who or what it was. No one thought to criticize or question. No one thought they were superior, because each being had its merits, although, as on Earth, there were none that were perfect. Not even Nebiré.*

*On Earth, in her true form, Nebiré knew that she would be considered a freak. Four arms, one, startling eye at the back and one at the front of her head and webbed feet would certainly have made her stand out from the human crowd.*

*So perhaps that question depends on where you are…*

For a while they rode in companionable silence, only remarking now and then on some feature of the landscape that caught one or the other's eye. Saddler was amazed by how relaxed he felt in this lady's company: they might almost have known each other for years.

After a while, by mutual consent, they decided to stop. It was getting very warm, and there was a small stream that looked as though it might be inviting for the horses.

Saddler sprang from his horse in much the same way as he had mounted, landing with a soft thud on the ground. The lady, however, rode to a nearby tree stump, where her horse stood patiently as she quite slowly dismounted.

Saddler was surprised. She rode so well and so lightly, that he had expected her to be able to dismount with equal ease. She turned from her horse and gave him a rueful smile, almost as though she guessed his thoughts.

Saddler blushed and, to hide his confusion, said: "Do you fink we should some'ow tether the 'orses?"

"They will be fine," was her reply.

And indeed, they were already grazing peacefully.

Saddler plumped himself down and leant back against the trunk of a large, majestic-looking tree. He watched as the lady came towards him and again was surprised by the rather ungainly way that she moved, as though walking was actually something of an effort for her.

Finally, she stood in front of him, hands on hips. She raised an enquiring eyebrow.

"Do you not yet know me, Saddler?"

He was about to reply, when she turned from him as if to look at the view. Her long golden hair shone in the sunlight and, as he watched, it parted slightly revealing a startlingly blue eye. Then the hair swung together again, and the eye was gone.

"Nebiré!" cried Saddler, leaping to his feet, tearfully flinging his arms around her. "You don't know 'ow glad I am to see you! But 'ow?"

Nebiré patted him on the back and motioned him to sit back down.

Watching her, Saddler realized how awkward her movements were, almost as though her body were not actually her own. Finally, seated beside him, she said: "Explanations will have to wait, Saddler. I cannot maintain this appearance for too much longer – it places a huge strain on both body and mind. I dare not risk my disguise slipping. I can, if need be, make myself invisible to the people here on Earth, although I would not be able to fool Crevitos. He would know in an instant that I was not from this world; the consequences would be disastrous."

Saddler looked at her with a complicated expression of both hope and desperation on his face.

"What must we do?" he asked miserably.

"First," said Nebiré, "tell me briefly how it is with you. What does Crevitos want? Have you fully regained your memory?"

There was a momentary silence. Then Saddler's face crumpled, and his shoulders heaved as the tears flowed unchecked down his anguished face.

# CHAPTER TWENTY-SIX
# SADDLER IN DESPAIR

*Back in the time before Anthony and Destiny had even known about Emajen, or gateways to other worlds, or Saddler, the thing that had bound them instantly as friends had been their love of animals.*

*Merlin was known to everyone who visited Grey's Ranch as a 'horse whisperer'. On her first visit to the ranch, Anthony had explained to Destiny that Merlin's approach with horses had nothing to do with whispering. It was all, he had told her, about psychology.*

*Destiny understood that. She was constantly learning to handle small animals in much the same way as Anthony was learning about horses. Merlin was a great teacher, but, as he himself said, if you didn't have a natural empathy, you could only learn so much theory.*

*Crevitos had quickly realised that Anthony and Destiny were somehow a key part of the attempt to save the Natorqua and prevent him from conquering Emajen.*

*What he hadn't banked on was just how powerful two young Earth beings could turn out to be…*

It had taken many long moments for Saddler to regain his composure. Nebiré had quietly lifted her gaze to the two grazing horses. Immediately they had stopped eating and come to stand beside Saddler where they resumed their steady munching once again. As always, their very presence was reassuring, and

Saddler had taken great comfort from their closeness. Finally, having taken several deep breaths to calm himself and wiped his eyes on his handkerchief, Saddler began to explain to Nebiré the dreadful catalogue of events, which had unravelled since he had been captured by Crevitos.

Much, of course, Nebiré already knew. There were times when Saddler had touched the ring in his pocket, so Nebiré had been able to reconnect with him. She was fully aware of the horrors he had seen in the mines of Doomland: she knew the torturous procedures through which innocent Creations were turned into mindless fighting machines. She had also seen many of the stages of Saddler's own development from being stripped of all his knowledge and memories to learning the very basics of walking and talking and becoming aware of the world into which he had been born, so to speak.

What Nebiré did not know was the exhausting battle Saddler was having with the demons inside his head. Demons that goaded him with unremitting thoughts of betrayal and evil doing.

*'All those Creations you have drawn Saddler – each and every one will suffer excruciating pain and misery because of you!'* they whispered constantly in his brain. *'You have become Crevitos's puppet. You will be the one who betrays your own people. It will be you who destroys your own world. How could you leave those children to die?'* And on and on and on…

There were also other demons which sought to persuade him that things were as they needed to be, that Saddler needed to look out for himself and that nothing he could do would change the fact that Crevitos could not be defeated.

All these thoughts raged a constant war inside Saddler's mind. He could not stop them. He thought he must go completely mad.

Head in hands, he shook his head from side to side and then looked up at Nebiré in despair.

"What can I do? I don't know 'ow much longer I can keep this up. Sooner or later, Crevitos is gonna work out that I'm only pretendin' to be 'is right 'and man. I'm no good. I'm useless. I've failed Emajen and you and Destiny and Anthony – everyone!"

Nebiré lay her hand on Saddler's shoulder.

"Look at me," she commanded strictly. Saddler raised his eyes helplessly to meet hers and for a moment was bathed in the soft, powerful glow that radiated from her one purple eye. He looked at her heart-shaped face and felt a gentle strength envelope him from head to toe. Then the image faded, and Nebiré's Earth form returned once more.

"Firstly," Nebiré said firmly, "You have no need to fear for Anthony and Destiny. Here…" Taking both of Saddler's hands in her own she closed her eyes, bidding him to do the same. In his mind's eye, he could see Anthony, Destiny and Boff packing up their belongings at the entrance to a small cave. It was clearly morning, though the sky seemed dull and lifeless. He watched as they began to scramble up a scraggy hill, then the vision faded.

"They continue their journey," Nebiré said simply.

Saddler took a deep breath before opening his eyes: "And 'ere's me moaning and finking of nobody but meself and all the while…" he choked on this thought, but suddenly there was a new determination in his voice and the demons seemed to have gone rather quiet inside his head.

"I 'ave to get back some'ow. I 'ave to 'elp 'em. I 'ave to 'elp save Emajen."

"And so you shall, but you cannot do this alone, Saddler, no single being could."

Delving deep into a pocket, Nebiré produced a purple-coloured stone.

"This crystal has energies that will help you fight off the destructive thoughts that beset you," she said.

"I cannot stay long, as you know, and I cannot protect you on Doomland, but this will help you to stay strong and to think more clearly in the dark times to come."

Just the thought of what lay ahead of him would have been too much for Saddler mere minutes ago. Now, he already felt strengthened. Nebiré also produced a small, ornate pouch which, she explained, contained his gateway back to Emajen when the time came.

"Choose wisely when you use it," she warned. "It only has the power to work once. When you return to Emajen, we must amass an army to resist Crevitos. I myself will send word the length and breadth of Emajen, so that we will waste no time once you return. For now, you must remain strong. Play Crevitos's game while you must. Anthony and Destiny cannot succeed without help and we cannot defeat Crevitos without the Natorqua. We can buy some precious time, perhaps, for Anthony and Destiny to connect with the Natorqua."

Saddler raised his chin. "I'm ready," he said.

Helping Nebiré to her feet, they mounted their horses once more. It was a quiet ride back to the ranch, each lost in their own thoughts of what had been and what was yet to come.

When they arrived at the stable yard, Crevitos was there, waiting. His raised eyebrow and slight smirk set Saddler's blood boiling, but he swallowed his irritation and merely looked at Crevitos enquiringly. Crevitos, as always, was in a hurry.

"I'm glad to see you're enjoying yourself," Crevitos said sarcastically. "Be quick now. We have much to do. We are done here."

Saddler ignored Crevitos for a moment. He turned and thanked Nebiré for a lovely ride. "I'll remember what you told me," he remarked with a smile.

Nebiré nodded. "Farewell, for now," she said.

Saddler turned back to tell Crevitos he would be right there, but Crevitos was already striding in the direction of their cabin. Saddler dismounted, thanked the ranch hand who was there to take his horse and thanked the horse for a lovely carry.

With one last look at Nebiré he hurried after Crevitos's rapidly retreating figure. Moments later, anyone watching their cabin would have seen a strange flash of light flicker at the window, immediately followed by an equally peculiar darkness.

# CHAPTER TWENTY-SEVEN
# DOUBTS RESOLVED

*Squib, as he was known to his friends, had been born on Earth. His early life had been very troubled: first losing his parents in a tragic accident and then being fostered by the dreadful Mr and Mrs M. Eanie.*

*When the Prof came across him, he'd run away and was scavenging cold chips out of a dustbin at a country fayre. The Prof had immediately taken Squib to a food tent and bought him a veritable mountain of food.*

*When the Prof had to leave, Squib had followed him, which was why he'd ended up on Emajen. Now he lived with the Prof, his bright little brain literally soaking up every nugget of information the Prof could impart - which was a lot.*

*He too had played his part in the saving of Emajen, and his loyalty to everyone in the this little group knew no bounds.*

*At heart, though, he was still a feral little thing…*

Going back to Doomland must have been so hard," Destiny said quietly.

"But at least he had hope," said Anthony.

"I fink," Saddler remarked quietly, "That this is about as 'ard as it gets. Wivout Nebiré I would 'ave failed you. I dunno what you all must think of me!"

Now that it was out, now that this part of Saddler's tale had been told, he felt two conflicting emotions in equal measure. It was a relief that everyone finally knew who he really was and how close he had come to betraying them and this very world he loved so much. Then again, he felt a deep sense of shame and embarrassment at his own weakness and, yes, he had to face it, his cowardice!

There was a stunned silence, during which everyone gazed open mouthed at Saddler. He wasn't one bit surprized by their reaction. He owed them his story, but now he was certain that they could never forgive him. Once his tale was told, it would probably be for the best if he left Emajen forever.

Such were Saddler's thoughts and so deeply was he immersed in them that he was taken by surprize when a small hand tentatively touched his arm. Bright, intelligent brown eyes gazed intently into Saddler's.

With unusual firmness in his small voice, Squib said simply: "I think you're a hero!"

At that there was an immediate clamour from the rest of the group. They gathered around Saddler, variously shaking his hand, patting his back, or hugging him. After a few moments, a flushed Saddler struggled to his feet, almost gasping for air.

"'ow could anyone want for better friends?" he said tearily.

Squib put his small hand into Saddler's much larger one and led him through the passage to the outside. The others followed.

They all stood for a moment drinking in the beauty of the scene through all their senses. It was warm, with just the hint of a gentle breeze that rustled softly through the trees and landed delicately on their skin. Above them the sky was blue, and all around them birds chattered and sang.

It was the kind of idyllic scene that you often read about in stories, but all too often didn't have time to stop and notice (let alone appreciate) on Earth.

Destiny linked arms with Saddler. Squib was looking at him intently, willing him to understand.

"I think Squib is trying to tell you that all is as it should be on Emajen, because of you," she said.

"Not me, not just me at any rate!" argued Saddler.

"No, as Nebiré said, we all played our part, but it wouldn't have worked without you! After all the dreadful things you've been through, we're just glad to have you back, safe and sound and still in one Saddler-sized piece!"

Destiny squeezed Saddler's arm and he gave her a grateful look. Suddenly, from nowhere, a quave appeared. It weaved around Destiny's legs for a moment and rubbed the side of its head lovingly against her calf. Then it gazed at Saddler and sprang lightly into his arms, where it settled comfortably and began to emit a throaty, rhythmic purr.

Although quaves were quite capable of talking, it wasn't something they did unnecessarily. Now this quave's actions spoke for themselves. Saddler was loved, not blamed. He was a good, brave, caring soul, and his fame on Emajen had spread far and wide.

"Quaves never lie!" remarked Nebiré.

For a while, the group stood about, absorbing the beauty of the day. Saddler's expression gradually softened. He began to relax as his breathing rose and fell with the quave's rumbling purr.

At some unspoken signal, the friends finally turned and made their way back into Nebiré's woodland home. Words had been spoken. Demons had been confronted. Bonds had been fortified.

But there was still a great tale to continue.

# CHAPTER TWENTY-EIGHT
# DEVASTATION

*To put no too finer point on things, Crevitos was a tyrant, a despot and a bully of the worst kind. Everything he did was either for the purely sadistic pleasure of seeing others suffer or was part of his plan to become the greatest ruler any world had ever known.*

*As a Creation, Doodland had been the unfortunate world upon which he had first tested his strength. It just so happened that Doodland was extremely rich in a substance called 'diamond'. This diamond substance was very pretty, but quite worthless, until Crevitos discovered a process by which it could be used to create an almost indestructible armour. From that point on, every inhabitant of Doodland not already in Crevitos's employ was set to digging in the mines.*

*It was a dreadful existence, as Saddler had discovered only too well…*

Back on Doomland, Saddler stood looking morosely out of the window. He was back in his room in the castle and the view from his window could not have revealed a greater contrast to the sights he had recently seen on Earth than if it had been hand-picked to do just that.

Before now, the withered landscape had been intriguing. With no other experiences or memories to draw on, Saddler had looked upon this outside space with no particular feeling at all.

Now he looked at the desolation and felt as though a tight fist had clamped around his heart, squeezing it tight until he could barely breathe.

He didn't know what Doomland had been like before, but he was pretty certain it was not like this. Surely, no planet inhabited by generally decent folk would look like this. They would tend to it and care for it wouldn't they? Just like everyone did on Emajen. Emajen - here his heart most definitely missed a beat. He missed it with an intensity that was close to unbearable.

Saddler's mind strayed to the visit Crevitos and he had made to the Amazon jungle: what a tremendously long time ago that already seemed now. In his mind's eye, the group they'd been with was standing by the base of a tremendous Tawari tree. The guide had been telling them about the incredible medicinal properties it possessed and how scientists had only as yet tested around 1% of all the medicines that could potentially be used to help to cure a whole multitude of ills.

Someone in the group had asked if de-forestation was a big problem where these types of medicines were concerned. Saddler had never heard of de-forestation, but it didn't sound good. He had listened carefully to the guide's reply and was horrified by what he'd heard.

Over the last hundred years, the guide had told the group, the rainforest had been (and still was being) destroyed at about 1.5 acres per second; this was roughly about the size of a football field. Per second! This had produced a gasp of horror, which had turned into a collective groan when the guide told them that 137 rainforest species were destroyed every day and that, because of this, 50,000 species a year could become extinct.

As if this wasn't enough, the guide had also explained that global warming, largely caused by rich nations, risked destroying vast amounts of the rainforest. Some scientists, it appeared, were of the opinion that if the world's temperature increased by only three degrees, then 75% of the Amazon would be destroyed.

"The Amazon Rainforest is not known as the lungs of the planet for nothing," he had said sombrely. "It provides about 20% of the world's oxygen. Imagine where we would be without it."

Back in his room, Saddler pictured himself asking the guide in a shocked voice why people would do that to their world. The guide had shrugged his shoulders. "Money," was what he had said. "It always comes down to money."

Saddler had the same feeling of desolation now as he'd had then. Why, oh why, would you not want to look after your world? Even if it was just for the selfish reason of making sure you still had a world to live on.

Looking out of his window, he could see the living proof (or perhaps not so living) of what war and greed and total carelessness had done to this planet.

Now it would appear that this was what Crevitos had in mind for Emajen.

Well, he wouldn't succeed! Not while there was a single breath left in Saddler's body to defend his beloved world.

He turned from the window just as the door to his room opened and Crevitos appeared.

"Come!" Crevitos said shortly. "Time is of the essence and there is much to be done."

Saddler gave one last look behind him at the ravaged landscape beyond the window and though his heart was leaden, he plastered a cheery expression onto his face as he followed Crevitos from the room.

# CHAPTER TWENTY-NINE
# THE MINES

*When Creations come alive on Doodland, they come in all shapes and sizes, colours and patterns - indeed, whatever the human mind can conjure up to doodle may come alive as a Creation.*

*Mostly, Creations tend to have similar personality traits to their creators (hence everyone's amusement when Destiny and Boff are together). There are some exceptions, of course. More complex Creations such as Crevitos are often fashioned with a particular purpose, or character in mind. Problems can arise, however, when humans discard their doodles and leave them to their own devices…*

Days followed; endless days they seemed, when Saddler spent the majority of his time in the mines. This was really difficult to gauge the right reaction to. He knew what went on in the mines, and any sane person's reaction would be to recoil with horror at the very thought of being there. But Crevitos, of course, believed that Saddler's memory was still clear of anything that happened before he took the potion. Saddler dared not even give the slightest hint that he knew what happened down there, or else the game would be up. His horror and revulsion might, with a gargantuan effort, be hidden from view, but how should he react when Crevitos took him down into the mines for the first time?

Crevitos was almost sending out sparks, so great was his energy. It occurred to Saddler that Crevitos would be highly amused by the opportunity to show off his dominion, and the atrocious activities within it, to Saddler for the first time. Except that it was the first time for the second time, so to speak. Crevitos knew that Saddler had seen it all before: he knew the disgust and loathing Saddler had felt. But as far as he was concerned, Saddler would have no memory of this. How would he expect Saddler to respond now? How would a Saddler with no experience of caring about, or for, others, react to what he was about to see? Would he be disgusted anyway? Would that be a response that came naturally to anyone, or would he be unmoved by the plight of the Creations toiling in the mines? Then there was this vile, inhuman process poor Creations went through where they were agonizingly layered with diamond armour, before having their minds erased so that they would become a part of Crevitos's almost indestructible fighting machine. Would Saddler be able to pretend that he wasn't horrified to his very core by this procedure?

As they descended the stairs for the first time on their way to the mines, Saddler had to think quickly. Not responding at all would be too hard. The strain would show in his face. In any case, it wouldn't be what Crevitos wanted. Crevitos wanted to either be amused by someone else's discomfort, or he wanted to be told how incredible his achievements were. If Saddler showed his disgust, Crevitos would not be able to trust him and then any chance of escape would vanish: he would be watched even more closely than he was watched now.

No, he would be interested and appreciative of Crevitos's brilliance. He would show willing to learn and to be involved. Perhaps if he acted a part, he would be able to keep his real feelings out of view.

Saddler remembered to be suitably impressed by the lift; it was an invention Crevitos had magpied from Earth. The first time Saddler had been in this one, it had taken his breath away, plunging several hundred feet into the very bowels of Doomland.

Although he was dreading this sensation again, Saddler carefully kept his expression neutral until the contraption began its descent. His cry of: "Oh!" was entirely genuine; he had actually forgotten how unsettling it felt to have the ground drop away beneath your feet. Fortunately, Crevitos took it to mean that it was an unexpected experience for Saddler. Saddler's reaction prompted one of Crevitos's cruel smirks.

"Impressive, eh?" said Crevitos.

"Wow!" was all Saddler could summon up the will to say. Apparently, this was praise enough from Crevitos's point of view.

Phew, passed that test, Saddler thought grimly to himself.

The mines themselves were every bit as appalling as he remembered them. Everywhere he looked, Creations of all shapes and sizes, stumbled and strained and wiped sweat and muck from their eyes as they worked ceaselessly to find diamond ore, Crevitos's secret ingredient for the tough armoured shell he literally welded onto other Creations in the bizarre and grotesque process that filled the cavernous mines with screams of pain and terror.

Knowing that this was a test bigger than any he had yet faced from Crevitos, Saddler surreptitiously took a deep breath to steady himself. Then he focussed his mind on asking questions; why was this done this way? What was this thing called? How long did it take to do such and such? He stored Crevitos's answers away carefully in his brain, knowing full well that it would not be enough just to ask the questions.

It would appear that Crevitos was deceived by his attitude; he answered all of Saddler's questions with no sense of irritation and, indeed, he seemed pleased by Saddler's interest.

The first day had clearly encouraged Crevitos to trust Saddler and the next few days involved Saddler learning details about every aspect of the operations going on in the depths of Doomland. Details Saddler dearly wished he didn't need to know; details that sickened and revolted him, even while he struggled to keep his expression unaffected and curious.

The only upside to the situation (if you could possibly call anything here an upside) was that Crevitos had not yet asked Saddler to begin drawing Creations again. The thought that he, Saddler, would be responsible for bringing poor creatures alive just so that they could be put through unbelievable torture by Crevitos, was intolerable.

Saddler could only hope that he would be able to find some way out before he was put to work drawing Creations once more.

# CHAPTER THIRTY
# DEVELOPMENTS

*Once Saddler had regained his memories, he very quickly realized that there were two things Crevitos desperately needed. Firstly, he needed someone strong to draw Creations for him. Secondly he needed to find a way to expand the gateway between worlds. Until now, individuals, or perhaps small groups had been able to use the mysterious boxes to travel from one world to another. It appeared that nobody, though, had succeeded in transporting anything like the size of the army that Crevitos had in mind.*

*Essentially, it was a race in time between Saddler finding his way home and Crevitos creating an army-sized gateway. As if things weren't bad enough for Saddler, this realization meant that now the pressure was really on…*

After a couple of days, Crevitos told Saddler that there had been developments. This being the case, he wanted Saddler to spend a couple of days on his own in the mines, making sure he understood every aspect of the work that was going on there. Crevitos didn't specify what these developments were, however, Saddler had a sneaking suspicion that it was to do with the gateway Crevitos's scientists were working on.

It occurred to Saddler that he must ready himself for action at a moment's notice. If Crevitos were likely to depart sometime soon, Saddler needed to use the time wisely. He desperately needed to make a connection between himself and some of the Creations working in the mines, for he would certainly need their help. This would be tough. Not only would the Creations be highly suspicious of him (and rightly so) thinking that he was one of Crevitos's right hand men, but he also had the problem of Snake to deal with.

Although Saddler had had very little to do with anyone on Doomland apart from Crevitos, he had been entrusted to Snake's care on one or two occasions. He didn't like Snake: Snake didn't like him. The feeling of dislike was, you might say, mutual. As was the feeling of mistrust. As far as Saddler was concerned Snake was pure evil. He didn't believe there was a single bone or cell in Snake's body which harboured any kindness or compassion for any other being. Essentially, Snake was a bully. He did as he was told by Crevitos because he was afraid. Then he took out his frustration and anger on the poor Creations under his control. Snake, for his part, was both suspicious of Saddler and jealous of him. Until Saddler came along, it had always been Snake who was number one in Crevitos's hierarchy. It was Snake who ensured that Crevitos's instructions were carried out to the letter. It was Snake who meted out punishment if orders were not obeyed, or sometimes even if they were.

In real terms, not much had changed: Saddler was not yet at the stage where he was given any command. But he was clearly

Crevitos's pet project. Snake didn't know exactly why this was, nonetheless, it rankled.

Also, Snake was not as convinced as Crevitos by Saddler's loss of memory. So, he watched carefully, waiting for his moment to catch Saddler out. In his warped and very limited imagination, Snake pictured the scene: Crevitos beside himself with rage at Saddler's betrayal, turning to the only other being that he could really trust.

"Deal with him!" Crevitos would snarl. And Snake would take the greatest delight in doing just that.

Slowly.

Painfully.

And then he, Snake, would command his rightful place by Crevitos's side once more.

For now, however, he made life as awkward for Saddler as he could, appearing as if from nowhere, seeking to catch Saddler unawares, whilst all the while pretending that he was only being helpful and looking out for Saddler.

Saddler found Snake nauseating and he was not fooled: this next couple of days in the mines, he would have to be very careful indeed!

# CHAPTER THIRTY- ONE
# CREVITOS DEPARTS

*Within the mines of Doomland, Creations toiled and were cruelly treated. They all knew what they were labouring for: they knew that the very diamond they dug up would be used on them and their friends, in a process that was vile and violent. And yet what choice did they have? Creations weren't strong by nature, and most could be easily erased. It wasn't much of a life, but at least they were still alive for now.*

*A few lucky ones like Boff managed to escape.*

*And the rest - well, they lived in hope…*

Two days later, before the tepid light that Doomland now called daylight had even begun to do battle with the pulsating darkness of the night, Crevitos and his entourage left the castle with a purposeful clatter of hooves.

From his window high above, Saddler watched. His heart was hammering as adrenalin coursed through his body. What he really wanted to do right this second, was to rush full speed down to the mines to begin to put in place the plan he had worked through, over and over again in his mind, until he was sure it was full proof. But part of that plan involved NOT doing exactly that.

If Saddler was up early watching Crevitos leave, then it was an absolute certainty that Snake would have been up earlier, fawning around Crevitos, assuring him that everything would be kept an eye on while he was away.

Saddler's hope had been that Snake would go with Crevitos. Crevitos, happy that Saddler now understood down to the last detail the workings of the mines and the whole operation around them, had charged Saddler with running the show, whilst he, Crevitos, was away.

Not only this, but Saddler must now work many hours a day drawing lethal Creations to swell Crevitos's army for when he returned.

But it was too much to hope that Crevitos trusted Saddler that much. Crevitos not only had intelligence of genius proportions, he also had a deviousness of equal magnitude. He was far too astute not to have realized that there was no love lost between Snake and Saddler.

By leaving them together, he was fairly assured that they would know that each was watching the other. The fact that they might also try to out-do each other in order to have greatest favour when he returned, also amused him greatly.

Of course, Crevitos didn't trust Saddler. He didn't trust Snake either. Crevitos trusted no one but himself, so this was, in his mind, the safest way to ensure the smooth running of things until his return.

So now Saddler waited. He watched the sad, eerie light of day creep through his window as he paced his room from one end to the other, knowing that however hard it was he must be patient. Snake must not have cause to suspect any hint of betrayal on Saddler's part, or he would instantly send word to Crevitos to return.

Finally, when it was as fully light as it was likely to be, Saddler sat himself down at the table Crevitos had prepared for him to do his drawings. The previous evening, he had quickly thrown together some sketches of Creations so that Snake would think he had been working since the early hours of the morning.

Having to draw Creations had been his greatest worry. He didn't want to be responsible for even one more creature's life of suffering, yet he couldn't see a way out of drawing them. It was Nebiré, again, who had come to his rescue.

"Leave one small part of each Creation uncompleted," she had told him. "It will need to be subtle, not immediately obvious to the eye. Make it your clear intention in your mind that each of these Creations cannot live until you – and you alone – finalize the drawing. Hopefully this will buy you enough time to evade giving life to any more of these poor creatures."

This advice had taken an immense weight off Saddler's shoulders. So far, he had not drawn much since they had come back from Earth and Crevitos obviously had too much on his mind to investigate whether any of Saddler's drawings had actually appeared on Doomland yet. Now, however, it needed to at least appear as though he were fulfilling Crevitos's orders.

Sure enough, it was not long before Snake's head appeared around the door.

"Ever 'eard of knocking!" Saddler remarked mildly, without looking up from what he was doing.

Snake didn't bother to comment. He was sneaky, but not particularly bright, and a clever retort was beyond him.

Instead, he strode across the room and leered menacingly over Saddler's shoulder, obviously hoping he would catch Saddler doing something he shouldn't be.

"Obviously never 'eard of personal space neither!" Saddler observed.

Disappointed, Snake adopted his most damning sneer and said: "These had better be good!" He marched back to the door and then turned to look at Saddler with an expression of pure loathing. "And it's time you were taking care of your duties in the mines!"

Saddler stretched with exaggerated care and sent an infuriatingly friendly smile in Snake's direction. "Right you are," he said smoothly. "Just finishing off, be there in a jiffy."

Snake looked as though he could cheerfully wrap his long, sinuous tail around Saddler's neck at this very moment. He might be stupid, but he had enough sense to know that he would never outwit Saddler when it came to a war of words. All he could do was to make it clear that he was going to watch Saddler's every move and at the first sign of anything dodgy on Saddler's part, Snake would be there to catch him at it.

Now all he could do was ensure that he had the last word.

"Make sure you are!" he said, before slamming the door swiftly behind him.

# CHAPTER THIRTY-TWO
# TAKING A CHANCE

*When Boff had first discovered a box in the mines of Doomland, he had seen it as no more than a welcome distraction. It was something he could hide that the guards didn't know about. It just made him feel as though he had a teensy, weensy bit of control over his miserable life.*

*Quite by accident, he had triggered the box's secret by opening it and saying a sentence containing the word 'imagen'. Perhaps it was that he hadn't spoken the word very clearly, or maybe it was just that 'Emajen' was the closest sounding place name, so that's where the gateway had taken him. It was something he would never know for sure, but he was jolly glad he had ended up where he had!*

*Not only was Emajen a wonderful world to live on, but he had also made some incredible friends. At the time, though, back when he had first arrived here, he had desperately wanted to use the gateway to help other Creations escape from their devastating existence on their doomed world. So that was exactly what he'd done...*

For several moments, Saddler surveyed the toil and bustle that was the essence of Doomland's mines. He would never cease to be disgusted and horrified by the fate of the Creations doomed to labour here hour after hour, day after day, until they were finally worn to nothing. However, he had very quickly perfected the face that he wore when he was down here with

Crevitos: now was no time to let his mask slip. Even if Snake himself wasn't in view, there were plenty of Crevitos's henchmen who would be under instruction to keep a close eye on Saddler's movements.

Adopting a nonchalant stance, Saddler strolled casually down one of the walkways and began, to all intents and purposes, to inspect what the various Creations were doing. This would be a pivotal moment. What he was now actually doing was watching the Creations carefully to see how they interacted with the guards.

Most Creations (he knew this from Boff) loathed Crevitos and everything he stood for. They would rather die than willingly help him. Sadly, this was too often the case. There were some, though, who saw service under Crevitos as the only means of escaping the torture and the terror that was the lot of the majority. There were some who would tell a tale just to make life a little easier for themselves. In other words, there were spies.

Saddler had to connect with some of the Creations down here; he had no choice. To do that, he would not only have to evade the ever-watchful eyes of Snake and his cronies, he would also have to pick the right Creation to talk to. Pick the wrong one, and his cover was blown. And that would be that.

So, he observed carefully. Every so often, whenever one of the guards was nearby, he would pick fault with some minor detail and soundly reprimand the poor Creation in question. He knew that it would be even more believable if he were to lash out and strike one or two, but he just couldn't bring himself to do it. There was enough violence going on in these mines as it was.

Time wore on interminably. It was just so hard. All the Creations looked equally dejected and exhausted – how could you tell if one were a spy?

He had to take the chance; there was no other option. Saddler headed for a cart being pushed towards one of the dumping shoots, by a small triangular-shaped Creation. Glancing around him briefly to check that he wasn't being observed, Saddler clapped a hand on the Creation's angular shoulder.

"You, there!" he said sternly. "I want to check this load."

The poor creation looked at him with frightened eyes and then hurriedly dropped its gaze. "Yes, Sir, of course, Sir!" it stammered.

Saddler bent down as if he were examining the bottom of the cart.

"BOFF!" he said to the Creation.

"P…p… pardon, Sir?"

For a second, Saddler's heart sank. It was a long shot, he knew, but it was the safest way he could think of to test where the Creation's loyalty lay.

Boff had a reputation amongst the genuine Creations; in fact, he was a bit of a hero. Saying Boff's name was really the only kind of proof Saddler had that he wasn't an enemy, and even that was sketchy. Among Crevitos's spies, he hoped that Boff's name was less well known.

"BOFF!" he said again more urgently, all the while apparently checking the cart. This time, the little triangular Creation clearly understood.

"We can't talk here, Sir," it whispered. "Watch me closely. I'll show you where. Say ten minutes?"

Saddler wasn't quite sure what alerted him to an approaching menace, a brief shadow perhaps, but he was instantly on his guard.

"Make sure you're more careful next time!" he snapped, raising his hand. The Creation cowered convincingly, but there was a definite brightness in its eyes that hadn't been there before.

"I'll be watching you!" Saddler said pointedly, as he brushed some imaginary rock dust from his clothes. He swept past Snake (who had obviously tried to sneak up on him) without a word.

For the next few minutes, he busied himself with various small jobs, all the while with one eye on the small triangular Creation and one on Snake. After a while, Snake appeared to be satisfied that Saddler was on task for the time being. He disappeared with one of the guards, no doubt to dish out more misery to some unfortunate Creation.

As soon as Snake had gone, Saddler looked for the distinctive triangle again. There it was, breaking huge rocks into smaller ones, along with two other Creations. Just at that moment, it glanced up at Saddler and, catching his eye, looked pointedly at an overhang of rock a few yards away.

What happened next, happened incredibly fast. Somehow, one of the Creations was now trapped under a vast pile of the broken rocks (Saddler suspected a small hole deliberately left for the Creation to crawl into). The other Creation was shouting and yelling and causing a tremendous commotion. There was only one guard around at that particular moment and as soon as he arrived at the scene, he was immediately surrounded by a whole gaggle of Creations shouting and pushing and generally causing mayhem.

Saddler reacted quickly. He couldn't see Snake, but in any case he had to grasp this chance with both hands. Under the cover of the chaos, he quickly dodged his way past the throng of Creations and slipped behind the overhang.

# CHAPTER THIRTY-THREE
# HATCHING A PLAN

*The caverns in the depths of Doomland, where Crevitos forced his slaves to toil, though huge in themselves, were only a part of the vast labyrinth of caves and passages that sprawled and snaked within its depths. Doodland was as old as time itself and many Creations from millennia past had sought to explore or make homes for themselves both on the planet and under its surface. No world, however great, is without its dark and hidden depths, and Doodland was no exception. Since Crevitos had become its ruler, that darkness had spread.*

*Still, Boff was hopeful that one day it would be restored to its former glory, and the evil that pervaded it now would be but a shadowy and distant memory…*

Behind the overhang, three Creations waited for Saddler to appear. As soon as he ducked around the side of the rock, the triangular comrade beckoned urgently, and they all swiftly retreated into the shadows at the very rear of the rocky protuberance. Greetings were rapidly exchanged - they were all well aware that there was no time for niceties.

"We're here because you used Boff's name." The triangular Creation, whose name apparently was Ting, addressed Saddler cautiously. There was bound to be uncertainty on both sides. Saddler could of course be setting a trap for the Creations; likewise, they might be setting a trap for him. With so little time at their disposal, someone had to take the plunge and show their hand. Someone had to reveal their true allegiance: you were either with Crevitos, or you were not!

Saddler figured he had nothing to lose. If these were genuine Creations, they would undoubtedly help him. If not...

"I'll tell it as briefly as I can, and then if you're wiv me, I'm gonna need your 'elp."

The Creations listened to Saddler's tale with growing concern and yet, at the same time, he could see them visibly relax, as they realized he must certainly be who he said he was. No one would bother to make up such an elaborate story just to ensnare a few miserable Creations.

Finally, Saddler said: "So you see, I need to get out of 'ere as quick as can be, before Crevitos comes back."

"Why not just use the gateway you've been given?" queried one of the other Creations. It had a rather bulbous, fish-like head, which was covered with incredibly delicate sparkly, multi-coloured fronds. In another place and time, Saddler would have been captivated by such a vision. He didn't have time to be captivated now.

"Number one, I'm gonna need as much time as possible before anyone realizes I've gone and using the gateway 'ere might attract too much attention. And two, Nebiré was worried about 'ow much strength a temporary gateway might 'ave on this world. She said better not risk it in the castle or the mines. Some'ow, I need to find a way out wivout anyone seeing me."

The other Creation, who was tall enough to have to stoop under the rear of the overhang, spoke up.

"There is an exit. It's one we use rarely when desperate measures are called for. But that takes you into the very bowels of the mines. It's a maze down there."

Ting shuddered involuntarily. "And there are untold horrors lurking in the dark recesses."

"We can draw Saddler a map. It's the only way he can leave here undetected," argued the tall Creation. "There are dangers, it's true." Here he looked at Saddler. "We will equip you as best we can. I don't see any other way."

Saddler closed his eyes for a moment and drew in a deep breath. Opening his eyes once more, he said: "If there's no other way, then it's what must be."

From beyond the overhang, the sounds of chaos were lessening. Their time was almost up.

“There’s one other fing I’m really gonna need your ‘elp wiv,” said Saddler, pushing all thoughts of his impending journey through the sinister depths of the mines to the very back of his mind. There would be time enough later to worry about that. For now, he had a more urgent matter to deal with.

“It ‘as to do wiv Snake,” he said grimly. “’Ere’s what I ‘ave in mind.”

# CHAPTER THIRTY-FOUR
# A MOMENT OF CALM

*Fortitude - dictionary definition: Courage in pain or adversity.*

*Courage - dictionary definition: the ability to do something that frightens one.*

*In Saddler's mind, he had shown neither courage nor fortitude during his time on Doomland. If anything, he felt he had been weak and cowardly. To his friends - indeed to anyone you might ever ask on Emajen - Saddler was a complete hero. He had experienced traumas none of them could even begin to imagine.*

*This, though, was why it was so hard for him to tell his story. He was afraid it would show him in what he saw to be his true light.*

*Strange how often it is the valiant who have no clue as to their own bravery…*

Back in Nebiré's room on Emajen, Saddler rubbed his eyes and looked wearily at the faces of those listening transfixed to his tale. They were dear friends, each and every one of them. Friends he could trust. Friends he had shared unbelievably dark times with. They understood with unwavering solidarity the need behind his personal quest. Now, here on Emajen, things were, for the most part, as they had always been. Life on Emajen had returned to the serene and harmonious state it had always enjoyed ever since time on this mystical world began.

The Natorqua, the very essence of Emajen, were at peace once more.

But, Crevitos had sought to ruin this. He had already turned Doodland into a barren wasteland, trapped its inhabitants into a life of abject misery and essentially destroyed the whole of that world. Unused to such evil and destructive desires, the inhabitants of Emajen had been bemused when Crevitos had begun to poison the Natorqua's minds, turning them into creatures of hatred and cruelty before, bit by bit, destroying the herd.

This was Saddler's world. Emajen was his home, his life – his very existence. His dear friends who had helped to defeat Crevitos understood his need to save his world.

Looking at them now, Saddler felt overcome with gratitude to them all. In a way though, it made it so much harder to tell them the next part of his tale. He was about to take them on a journey that was probably best left locked in the furthest, darkest oubliette of his mind.

They had all been through so much, he didn't want to take them there and yet he must.

And here was Squib handing him a much-appreciated cup of nutty tasting Emajen tea. The cure for all ills, his dear old mum would say. Thinking about her made Saddler smile. She was blissfully unaware of exactly what had happened to him. Proud as punch, of course (as only a mum can be) of his part in saving

Emajen. It was restful, though, that he didn't have to think too much, or explain too much, when he was with her…

Everyone was talking quietly. The tea had had its usual soothing effect. Squib was busying himself with some errand for Nebiré, Destiny was (unsurprisingly) fussing over Kaz, and Boff and Anthony were discussing some latest invention of the Prof's.

Saddler sipped his tea slowly, grateful for this short interlude in his storytelling.

This was what they had all fought for. And if he could not share his story with such wonderful friends, friends who had been – and would continue to be – with him every step of the way, then whom?

Squib appeared at his elbow once more. He patted Saddler's shoulder gently with one small hand and took Saddler's empty mug with the other.

'Such incredible empathy in one so young,' thought Saddler. And Squib's quick, almost answering smile gave Saddler the strength to carry on.

# CHAPTER THIRTY-FIVE
# PLANS

*Snake. An evil creation and therefore much valued by Crevitos. How Snake would have loved to be top dog instead of Crevitos! Unfortunately for Snake, all Creations have some characteristics in common with their human creators. The young artist who had doodled Crevitos was not far short of genius. Snake's human - well, let's just say, he was not quite in the same league.*

*Even so, Snake was robustly drawn, and the long tail he possessed that had given him his name was a formidable weapon. He might not have had the vast intellect of Crevitos, but he was devious and sneaky. It was no wonder that he was regarded by all other creations with a mixture of fear and hatred…*

The plan was this, and it was very simple. Ting, being an extremely brave little Creation, would approach Snake with a wildly excited story about Saddler being in trouble; and, moreover, in a part of the mine in which he had no real reason to be. The hope was that Snake's obsession with catching Saddler out would stop him thinking too hard or questioning too much. What they wanted was for Snake to follow Ting into a quiet part of the mine, where Saddler would be supposedly injured and unable to defend himself.

Snake, of course, was incredibly strong, so he would need to be caught off his guard. As soon as he approached Saddler, then a whole gang of other Creations would appear from the shadows. If Snake could be overpowered (and it was a big if) he could be stowed somewhere safe from the prying eyes and ears of the other guards, allowing Saddler to make his escape.

Having thought about it all very carefully beforehand, Saddler had concluded that the time to do this would be just after the night workers began their shift. This was something that Snake always oversaw. He was also a creature of habit. Once the shift had changed, he would meet up with some of the others to play a game of Doom, before retiring to his quarters for the night.

If Ting approached him just as he was settling to his game, Snake would hopefully be annoyed enough to react without thinking. If he didn't return, the others would no doubt assume that he had dealt with the problem and gone straight to his room. This would give Saddler the whole night, at the very least, to affect his escape, before anyone even began to look for Snake.

"Maybe you'd better come wiv me," Saddler said pointedly to Ting. "When they find Snake, 'e's goin' to be lookin' for someone to punish. And no disrespect like, but 'e's not goin' to forget in a hurry that it was you 'oo tricked 'im!"

"I've thought of that." Ting looked quite pleased with himself. "I'll go the opposite way to you and leave a not too obvious trail. Just to create a bit more confusion and buy you some more time.

Then at some point, I'll double back – they'll be left with no more trail to follow!"

"That's a splendid plan," said Saddler, "But at some point, Snake's still goin' to find you and I don't like to fink what 'e might do when 'e does."

"Oh, I have a handy little feature that I think might just do the trick." Ting turned his back on Saddler, who watched him curiously. After a few seconds, Saddler said, "I can't see no…" just as Ting turned back to face him. A Ting with very distinctive yellow colouring, decorated with vivid orange spots. As Ting was normally a rather pretty mauve colour, the change was quite startling.

"I can't do it for too long," said Ting. "It begins to fade after a little while, but it's what Snake will see and remember. He won't be looking for a Creation my colour and I'm certainly not the only Creation of this shape."

"Ingenious!" Saddler was impressed. He shook the little Creation soundly by the hand and then watched mesmerized, as Ting took a deep breath and held it. He held it for so long, that Saddler began to feel quite alarmed, but just as he was about to forget the whole plan and shout for help, Ting change colour again with a soft 'plop' and he smiled at Saddler triumphantly.

To give Ting time to enlist the help of some other Creations, they all decided that the following evening would be the time to act. It was a necessary delay, but even though Saddler knew this, he was anxious to get started.

The time seemed to slow almost to a standstill. There was nothing now that he, Saddler, could do. It was all in the hands of his new comrades. All he could do was wait.

# CHAPTER THIRTY-SIX
# A NICE CUP OF TEA

*Crevitos had been pleased with the way Saddler had shaped up. It had been an excellent idea of Snake's to take Saddler on a trip to fuel his imagination. Even so, Crevitos didn't believe in praise, or loyalty. He knew only too well that Snake's faithfulness was born out of fear. It amused him to think that Snake would overthrow him in a flash if he ever got the chance. That opportunity would never present itself though, because Snake would never be clever or brave enough to seize the moment should it arise.*

*Saddler now - well, he was a different kettle of fish altogether. He was biddable and quick, but - and here was a bit of a stumbling block - whilst the potion may have eradicated his memories, it hadn't changed his essential character. Saddler lacked even the slightest hint of meanness or cruelty, and whether that would eventually turn out to be a problem, Crevitos had no way of knowing. Still - and here, Crevitos allowed himself a wry smile - Snake would ensure Saddler towed the line while he, Crevitos, was away…*

Saddler sought to keep himself busy for the interminable hours until the day shift ended, and the night shift began.

Surprisingly, he had slept well that night; no doubt he was exhausted by the emotional turmoil of the previous day. He had awoken feeling refreshed and ready for whatever the next step of this bizarre journey held in store for him.

As he made his way down to the mines, he wondered how he should play things for the next few hours. It occurred to him that it would be a good idea to arouse Snake's suspicions just a little, so that when Ting approached him that evening Snake would be more than ready to believe his tale.

So, what would make Snake even more wary of Saddler than he already was? If he, Saddler, were to be rather friendly with some of the Creations, be seen being rather chatty to them, say, that would certainly give Snake pause for thought.

But no, it was too risky. The Creations themselves might end up getting into trouble.

No. Not a good idea. So then, maybe, if he approached it the other way: if he was excessively mean and angry, Snake would definitely smell a rat. He knew only too well that Saddler was soft with the Creations. Any show of aggression from Saddler would be out of character.

Yes, that was probably the way to play it. The Creations and Saddler had already agreed that they would know each other by a very simple sign. They would smile. Creations in the mines didn't even dare to have eye contact with their oppressors; they certainly didn't smile. Saddler would just have to approach one or two of his co-conspirators and make a show of being really vicious at a time when he knew Snake was watching. The Creations themselves would understand, and he hoped that Snake would be just doubtful enough to think that Saddler was up to something.

Saddler had just reached the bottom of the stairs leading to the lift, when he ran bang, smack into Snake himself.

"Watch where you're going," Snake hissed. His forked tongue flicked rapidly across his lips and his tail twitched in its pouch, as though it would love to throttle Saddler there and then. Up until this point, Saddler had always been studiously polite to Snake. Now he adopted what he hoped was a mean expression.

"Oaf!" he snarled, as he pushed Snake roughly out of the way. He fully expected Snake to retaliate. A full-blown fight between them now though would wreck all his carefully laid plans, but he surprised himself by feeling ready for just that.

For a split second, Snake looked taken aback. The moment teetered. Both watched breathlessly to see which way it would fall.

It rocked and overbalanced.

Much to Saddler's surprise, Snake laughed.

"Oaf, yourself," he said lightly. "Clearly someone got out of the wrong side of bed this morning."

Saddler merely grunted. He turned his back on Snake and stomped angrily towards the lift: despite his, by now, genuine annoyance, he would have been rather gratified to see the look of sly loathing and suspicion in Snake's almond-shaped eyes.

Inside the lift, his pulse was racing. It was all he could do to control the shaking that threatened to turn him into a quivering jelly.

As the heavy iron gate to the lift clanged shut behind him, he sank to the floor with his head in his hands.

What had happened to him? What was he becoming? The old Saddler would never have provoked a fight; would never have believed he even had it in him. And was that rage he had felt? The Saddler who ambled through life taking joy from every smallest moment, seemed to be melting into a mere blob of the past.

Well, he didn't like this new Saddler. He didn't like the way these emotions made him feel. And what would Mrs Saddler say if she could see him now? Just what?

"You know what, Saddler me old son – you know very well what she'd say," he told himself. "She'd say, up you get Saddler me love. No use moping. What's got to be done, has got to be done. Buck up now dear one, when it's all sorted, we'll 'ave a nice cup o' tea."

"A nice cup o' tea," Saddler repeated to himself. "That sounds grand. Come on lad," he told himself, "Mrs Saddler's right. You got a job to do, so best be doin' it. You're up to your neck in it now, so nuffin's to be gained by feeling sorry for yourself."

Saddler stood up and brushed the inevitable mine dust off his clothes. He had a world to try to save and if he wasn't quite the same old Saddler at the end of the proceedings, well maybe that was to be expected. If he wasn't the same, at least he would still be alive. If he failed – well, then it wouldn't really matter…

Either way he was pretty sure he'd rattled Snake: Saddler allowed himself a grim smile at his own joke.

By the time the lift reached the bottom of the shaft, Saddler's resolve was exactly where it needed to be.

He slid open the vast iron gate and stepped resolutely out into the mine.

# CHAPTER THIRTY-SEVEN
# SETTING THE SCENE

*Cruel - definition: wilfully causing pain or suffering to others or feeling no concern about the pain others feel.*

*Crevitos was cruel, there was no doubt about that at all. He didn't care about causing anguish and misery to the Creations who toiled slavishly in his mines. Not only that, it actively amused him when his henchmen were cruel. To Crevitos, the inability to be mean to others who were in your power was weakness at the very least. He had to admit it was an aspect of Saddler's character which could be considered a flaw. However, Saddler's main purpose was to draw strong Creations, so perhaps it was of no importance.*

*And, of course, Saddler's mind was still relatively young and malleable…*

As he travelled around the mine, Saddler was greeted by a number of cautious smiles. Actually, it was really heart-warming. All his life he had taken the cheeriness and jolliness of those around him on Emajen for granted. The first time he had encountered any really negative attitudes, was on his first visit to Earth. After a while of watching people rushing here and there, always it seemed in a panic to be somewhere else, or doing something different, he wasn't altogether surprised that they were miserable and stressed. Why would you spend your living time doing things you hated and being in a tremendous rush to get onto something else you hated even more? The whole approach to life on Earth baffled him. Then he had visited Grey's Ranch and it had almost been like coming home.

Now, here in the mines of Doomland, he felt his spirits lifted by the careful smiles of those who had agreed to help him. He experienced a new surge of determination. He was not alone in his quest to defeat Crevitos. When he finally made it to Emajen (and make it he would) he knew the others would be waiting for him. He knew, too, that he had Nebiré's considerable mind strength on his side. And now, it was not just about saving Emajen, but also about helping these poor Creations to turn Doomland back into their beloved Doodland again.

Saddler occupied himself by seeking out his comrades and making a great show of finding fault with everything they were doing. Each time, he would throw them an agonized glance and whisper, "I'm so sorry to 'ave to do this."

The understanding nods and winks that he received in return made him feel even worse.

Snake had reappeared in the mines not long after Saddler; he was clearly on the lookout. Every time Saddler took an unfortunate Creation to task, Snake seemed to be somewhere close by, keeping a watchful eye on things.

The Creations themselves played their part with tremendous gusto. They whimpered. They cowered. They grovelled. Saddler could almost believe they were quite enjoying themselves. He couldn't though quite bring himself to really lash out and cause actual pain to anyone, and it soon became obvious that Snake was losing interest, since clearly nothing untoward was happening.

Finally, Saddler came across Ting who was wearing his best yellow and orange disguise.

"I'm not arousing 'is suspicions enough," Saddler hissed. He threw a glance in Snake's direction.

"You need to be horribly, horribly angry!" Ting whispered back as he cowered convincingly away from Saddler's fake menacing expression. "Big Creation over there. Four big feet. See?"

Saddler shifted his position and roared loudly at Ting to cover the fact that he was looking for the Creation Ting had pointed out.

"Gotcha!"

"He's got scales all over, under his clothes. If you strike him, he won't feel a thing."

"Fanks! I 'ate doing it though!"

"We know! Go quickly, Snake's on his way."

"Useless Creation!" Saddler bellowed. He raised his whip as though to strike Ting, who whimpered convincingly. There was a sneer on Snake's face though, as Saddler lowered his whip without striking.

Pretending that he had no idea of Snake's appearance behind him, Saddler made a great show of being totally incensed by something another Creation was doing (or not doing) across the mine. He strode in the direction of the four-footed fellow, bellowing; "OY! You!" at the top of his voice.

The Creation in question shuffled all four feet clumsily around so that he was able to throw a knowing smile in Saddler's direction, without being seen by Snake, who was watching interestedly now from a slight distance.

Saddler's stomach cramped. He knew what he needed to do, and it made him feel sick.

"'Ow many times, you idiot? This ain't the first time me and you's 'ad words." Without giving himself even the slightest pause for thought, Saddler brought his whip slashing down around the poor creature's back. The Creation crumpled and doubled up in pain so convincingly, that Saddler's heart skipped several beats.

"Be more careful next time!" he yelled.

He gave the poor creature a resounding kick before he stomped away. Reaching an overhanging piece of rock, that afforded privacy from prying eyes, he promptly vomited.

Across the mine, Snake's initially shocked expression had turned into one of thoughtfulness. He watched until Saddler disappeared from view, then he turned on his heal, too preoccupied to pay any attention to the Creations watching him warily as he marched away.

# CHAPTER THIRTY-EIGHT
# PREPARATIONS

*As his story progressed, Saddler found he was filled with conflicting emotions. All of them had been adamant that they thought of him as nothing short of a hero and reassured him that he had absolutely nothing to be ashamed of.*

*He was grateful for that - more so than they could ever realise!*

*However, there was still a way to go with his story and whilst there were parts that he even felt a little proud of, there was yet more that he cringed to remember.*

*He hoped against hope that all his friends' kindness and understanding would withstand the horrors yet to come...*

This was it. This was what all the preparation over the last day had been leading up to. Saddler had watched carefully, as Snake and his underlings had begun to herd the hoard of day workers into the carts that would take them up and out of the mine. It had been a sensible choice of time to affect the next part of the plan. It was the only time that Snake would be too absorbed to be aware of Saddler's actions.

"Quick!" Ting had appeared at Saddler's side. He had adopted a slightly murky brown-grey colouring that blended admirably with the rocky scenery around him. Saddler doubted that Snake would have been able to see Ting from that distance, even if he had had the time to look in their direction.

Ting tugged at Saddler's arm. "We have to go. Follow me, I'll show you where."

With one last glance back at the oblivious Snake, Saddler hurried after Ting, afraid that he would lose sight of the little fellow with his amazing camouflage.

After several twists and turns through rocky passages, that all looked alarmingly the same, Ting finally stopped in a fairly sizeable cave. For just a brief moment, Saddler was beset by a feeling of dismay. Could this all be an elaborate plan of Snake's to lure Saddler somewhere and then conveniently lose him, or worse still ensure that he would never be seen again?

"You're bein' paranoid old son," he muttered to himself.

Just then, Ting said: "All clear!"

From the deepest shadows of the cave, emerged a band of Creations. Although he had been surrounded by them in the mines, it still took Saddler's breath away to see so many wonderfully diverse features, colours, shapes and sizes, all smiling and coming forward to pat him on the back and shake his hand.

At once his fears subsided and he felt his resolve to help these wonderful beings return with renewed strength.

"I can't fank you enough for all your 'elp!" he said sincerely.

Just then, a rather rotund Creation with large, feathery ears came puffing into the cave. "The carts are loaded. Snake is on his way up to the guards' quarters," he said.

"Right then, we must get ready," Ting announced firmly.

Quickly, he showed Saddler a pile of rocks in a far part of the cave. It was shadowy enough for Saddler to sit behind the rocks as though he were trapped.

As Saddler settled himself into position, the Creations fussed over him, asking if he was OK and as comfortable as it was possible to be given the situation.

"I'm fine. You guys are something else again." Saddler laughed in spite of the serious circumstances.

As a finishing touch, the large four-footed Creation Saddler had unwillingly whipped, carefully piled a number of rocks on top of Saddler's legs as though he were completely wedged.

"Do forgive me!" The Creation worked quickly, but with incredible tenderness.

"Ain't nothing compared to what I did to you." Saddler looked at the Creation admiringly. After all they had been through – still were going through – these beings had only kindness in their hearts. It made him feel very humble. Ting, who was obviously in charge of the operation, rubbed dust off his hands and nodded, satisfied.

"Looks good. Time we were off."

Creations melted out of sight with a well-versed ease that suggested perhaps it wasn't the first time they had done so. Apart from a lamp which was placed carefully on its side just out of Saddler's reach, as though he had dropped it, the cave went dark. Dark and silent. All Saddler could do was wait.

# CHAPTER THIRTY-NINE
# BAIT

*When Boff began listening to Saddler telling the story of how the Creations on Doomland had helped him to escape, he was filled with pride. This was for two reasons. To begin with, he was elated that so many Creations had shown such courage in the face of real adversity. After all, he'd had firsthand experience of working in the mines and he knew what an exhausting and soul-destroying life the Creations there led. He also knew how incredibly hard it must have been for those Creations who'd helped Saddler, to stay behind. They had known how much more likely it would be that Snake could track a group rather than Saddler alone, and so they had stayed – even knowing what some of them might have to suffer as a consequence…*

It was impossible to tell in the darkness how much time had elapsed. It seemed both short and long – a strange phenomenon that darkness alone has the power to achieve. Perhaps he had even dozed – Saddler couldn't be certain - but one moment everything was black and still and the next there was light, commotion and uproar.

And there was Snake leering at him from the entrance to the cave, his expression thunderous.

"I KNEW you were up to no good…"

"I… I can explain!" Saddler stammered, hoping he would sound both guilty and afraid at being caught out.

"Really!" Snake's tone dripped sarcasm. "You no doubt have some elaborate story about searching for new seems of diamond ore, or something."

Saddler opened his mouth and closed it again as though that was exactly what he had been going to say. Snake surveyed the cave.

"Funny that." His almond-shaped, yellow eyes narrowed to mere slits. "This looks like a BARE CAVE to me!"

Saddler gulped. Snake had always been sly and creepy; now he was positively menacing. Danger and evil radiated from him in waves that made Saddler physically gasp. In that second, he feared all was lost. Surely, he and the small band of Creations hovering in the shadows would be no match for this snake-man with his forked tongue, venomous fangs and deadly coiled tail.

Except that it wasn't coiled any longer. In the blink of an eye, it had unravelled itself from the pouch at Snake's side and was now quivering ominously in Snake's hand.

Things happened fast.

Snake strode towards Saddler, and it didn't look as though his intention was to be helpful. In his panic to scramble out from beneath the pile of rocks and stones, Saddler's boot became snagged on a sharp rocky spur jutting out from the cave wall.

Saddler struggled to free himself. Snake rapidly closed the distance between them.

Abruptly, Creations erupted from all sides and threw themselves at Snake's threatening form.

He cast them off like insignificant specks of dust, his tail whipping left and right with violent abandon. Creations thudded against the rough walls of the cave and lay sprawled senseless on the dusty floor.

Saddler struggled vainly with his boot. Then he stopped and looked up helplessly as Snake leered over him.

"No one tries to get the better of Snake and lives to tell the tale!" Snake lisped with soft menace in his voice. His tail twitched. It rose slowly and hovered over Saddler, poised to strike.

"You sure about that?" a gruff voice queried from behind Snake.

Before Snake could react, a vast hand grabbed hold of his tail and thrust it to the ground. An even larger foot – one of four – stamped on the tail and pinned it there. Saddler meantime had managed to wriggle his foot clear of the trapped boot. As Snake twisted around to deal with his attacker, Saddler hefted up the biggest rock he could lay his hands upon and brought it crashing down on the side of Snake's head. Snake toppled and fell. Creations, already picking themselves up from the dusty floor hurried to assist, pinning Snake down so they could bind him tightly.

Then it was over.

Snake lay trussed and unconscious on the cave floor. There were smiles and hugs all round.

"'Es gonna 'ave an 'ell of an 'eadache when 'e comes round," Saddler said unsympathetically. Everyone laughed. "What now?" Saddler queried more seriously.

"Now," said Ting, "You need to get going without delay. We'll take care of Snake – it will be our pleasure!"

So saying, he handed Saddler a map and a backpack and with many wishes of good luck from the group, Saddler headed into the depths of the mines.

# CHAPTER FORTY
# CONCERNING SNAKE

*Although the Prof had lived on Emajen for many years and was no stranger to the more mystical side of life, there was still much about other worlds that mystified and enthralled him. For example, until Boff had found his way to Emajen with the box containing a gateway that he'd found in the mines, the Prof had never heard of a world where human doodles came into being. Since that time he'd learnt much about how Doodland worked from Boff, but he was still fascinated by the actual physical and mental attributes of the Creations who lived there. The fact that Creations could take on some of their creators' characteristics, for instance. How did that work? And Creations had tremendous stamina, as they'd demonstrated in the mines. Yet Crevitos wasn't strong enough to draw his own fighting Creations. It was all thoroughly intriguing…*

Looking at Saddler's face, Destiny could see that the telling of this last episode had really drained him. She glanced across to Nebiré, only to find that the mystic's gaze was already on her. Nebiré nodded almost imperceptibly at Destiny – a clear signal that for now Saddler's tale must remain where it was.

Destiny swallowed her disappointment. This last part of Saddler's recount had been so fraught and dramatic, that even she felt quite exhausted just listening to it. Imagine how Saddler must feel having to relive it all again.

"Do you know what happened to Snake?" she asked lightly.

Saddler gave a wan smile. "Over to you Boff," he said.

"Ah, yes." Boff's lightbulbs flashed. They darkened for a brief moment and then brightened again as though conflicting thoughts had flickered across his brain.

"I heard later on, from Ting, that there was a defunct well a little further on in the mine. They rather unceremoniously dragged Snake to it, and Ron – that's your four-footed friend, Saddler – dropped him in. None to gently either, I should say."

"Did they ever find him?" This came from Squib – curious as ever.

"Well, yes and no. Actually, what your friends hadn't considered, Saddler, was just how handy Snake was with his tail. After he awoke, it would seem that he managed to cut through the ropes he was bound with, by rubbing them against a jagged piece of rock. The well was pretty deep, but apparently, he used his tail to find crevices and footholds to hoist himself out."

"So, no one actually found him then?" Anthony queried.

"By that time, they were looking, and Snake had exhausted himself climbing out of the well. They found him passed out right on the edge."

"So what happened then?"

"When Snake came to again, he immediately insisted on a search party being sent out to trace Saddler. They found Ting's carefully laid trail, but then of course it led them round in a big circle to exactly where they'd started. By that time, you were long gone, Saddler."

With his typical no-nonsense honesty, Squib posed the question that was on everyone's lips, yet no one wanted to ask.

"Snake must have been so mad! What did he do then?"

Boff's lightbulbs darkened briefly as they had done before. Here was the part that didn't bear thinking about. With a tremendous sigh, he said: "Apparently, Snake's tail was pretty much shredded, and he was in such a state that the false trail sent him into a complete frenzy. He couldn't identify any of the Creations in the cave, since he'd had his back to them, but he remembered Ting alright. He had everyone on the lookout for a triangle-shaped Creation with yellow colouring and orange spots. He didn't find him, of course, but the others took great care to keep Ting out sight, even so. Snake was livid. "I'm afraid," here Boff shot an apologetic look at Saddler "… well, let's just say things didn't get any easier for the Creations in the mines after that."

"But," Destiny said hurriedly, "If Saddler hadn't escaped, Doodland would still be Doomland and under Crevitos's rule. So, it had to happen, right?"

"Yes, yes, it was a necessary evil," Boff agreed. "Fortunately, not long after that, Crevitos returned to say that the gateway was ready. Then it was all hands-on deck to prepare the army for the journey there."

"Well, what did Crevitos say? He must have been pretty miffed at Saddler's disappearance," said the Prof.

"That was the odd thing." Boff shook his head, bemused. "Of course, we'll never know what happened between him and Snake, but as far as Ting and the others could tell, he just seemed to shrug it off as a nuisance. He questioned the guards who were on duty that night, of course, but one of our spies in the Crevitos camp overheard him say 'No matter. He won't get far.' And that was the last we heard of it. I guess he had more important things on his mind."

"Like world domination!"

"Quite!"

"And what became of Snake?"

"I can answer that," Saddler said grimly. "He was at the battle alright, but I could see 'e was a shadow of 'is former self."

"Did you?"

"Yup!"

"Oh!"

"This was a side to Saddler that it was difficult to reconcile with the character they knew and loved. As if he understood this, Saddler continued, "If it 'elps, 'e looked as peaceful at the end as any of the others. Remember, 'e was a Creation too. Wasn't really 'is fault, being the way 'e was. Not everyone creates with love in their 'earts." He looked pointedly at Destiny and then at Boff. Boff's lightbulbs turned pink, a strangely similar shade to that of Destiny's cheeks. Glancing at Nebiré again, Destiny saw that it was time for them to go. This time, she was glad. Saddler's tale obviously had some way to go, and it was evident that there was more trauma for Saddler to relive in the tale to come.

Time for a break. Tomorrow, Saddler would be rested, and he would be ready to resume his dark, solitary journey through the vast labyrinth of Doomland's mines.

# CHAPTER FORTY-ONE
# ALONE

*Saddler now knew that there were worlds where wars happened all the time, Earth being no exception. Having lived all of his life on a world where such a thing had once been unthinkable, he still found it hard to believe what had happened on Emajen. What was incredible, was how quickly Emajen and its inhabitants had settled back into the comfort of the gentle life they had always known. Of course, the battle of Emajen was the source of great storytelling, and there was a tremendous sense of pride in how everyone had come together and fought to save their world from Crevitos's tyrannical grasp.*

*But Saddler knew he would never again be the same carefree fellow he had been once upon a time. What he had been through had changed him, and there was a part of him that would always wonder, always be afraid: was it possible that Crevitos was alive and well somewhere and plotting multi-world domination again?*

Saddler's lamp gave him just about enough light to follow the path in front of him. The first part of his route was simple enough; it ran straight and relatively smoothly for some considerable time, and Saddler knew from the map that he had to ignore all minor paths branching from the main one.

He quickly left all sounds of the others behind. Soon, it began to feel as if he were almost gliding through a dream. The dark shadows and the silence were disorientating and, before long, he lost all sense of how long he had been walking. After a while, the path began to slope steadily downwards. The ground itself became rougher, and several times Saddler stumbled on a loose piece of rock unseen in the gloom.

"Steady on Saddler, me old lad," he told himself sternly. "Ain't no one 'ere to 'elp if you take a tumble!"

Truth to tell, Saddler had never felt so alone and isolated in all his life. He tried whistling to himself to dispel the quiet, but the noise echoed eerily off the walls around him, and he thought on the whole that the silence was preferable.

After what seemed like an interminable time, the path began to level out, and he came to a point where the route branched in three directions.

In the brief time that Ting had had to show Saddler the map, he'd advised Saddler to take the left-hand fork.

"It's a longer way, but it's safer. For a while, you might think you're going back on yourself, but you're far more likely to exit the mine without any, shall we say, challenges on route."

He hadn't specified what those challenges might be, and Saddler hadn't asked. He would either deal with any challenges as he met them, or he wouldn't. No point in worrying about things before they happened.

The right-hand route was, apparently, virtually impassable. Rock falls had reduced the tunnel to crawling room only in some places and there was every possibility it might be completely blocked by now.

"It's a pity," Ting had told him. "It used to be the quickest and most direct route. We have a feeling it might have been deliberately sabotaged."

"What about the third way?" Saddler queried.

Ting had vigorously shaken his head. "Forget it even exists! There are things down there you do not want to meet. It's even been named the path of Doom! You'd be as likely to survive trying to walk out of the castle in full view of the guards."

"Not much choice then!" Saddler had said as he tucked the map carefully into his pocket.

It had seemed quite straight forward then, back in the relative brightness of the mines, with friendly Creations all around him. Now Saddler didn't much like the look of any direction. With only thick, black nothingness extending in front of him whichever way he looked, none of the paths were exactly inviting.

Saddler shivered. Although the descent hadn't been steep, he'd obviously come far enough down into the depths of Doomland for the temperature to have noticeably dropped. Hitching up his trousers which seemed to have become uncharacteristically loose since he came to Doomland, Saddler took a few hesitant steps into the left-hand tunnel. It was slightly narrower than the one he had just left, and there seemed to be other smaller tunnels branching off almost every few steps he took. He would have to be extremely careful to remain on the main route. In the darkness, it would be all too easy to step slightly to one side or the other and end up on a path to who knows where.

Concentrating with such intensity on the way before him was a strain. Not being able to relax for a single moment began to take its toll. Saddler realized he was going to have to stop for a bit to regain his strength. His stomach was rumbling too: he had no idea how long it was since he had last eaten – certainly some hours ago.

Saddler held his lantern aloft and peered cautiously into each of the openings as he passed. Finally, he found an opening that wasn't another tunnel, but a niche hewn into the rock, with a low slab clearly designed to be sat on. Ting had told him he would find a few of these along the way.

"Rest whenever you can," he'd said. "It's an arduous journey. I can't really explain, but you'll see."

And see, Saddler did. The slab was hardly the height of comfort, but just now it felt like the most wonderful, restful place he had ever encountered. Saddler sat for a moment resting his head back against the harsh wall. He closed his eyes for just a second and his head span with all the crazy events of the day. Then Saddler slept.

# CHAPTER FORTY-TWO
# HOPE AND DESPAIR

*Listening to Saddler's description of the mines of Doomland brought it all back to Boff. After Destiny had doodled him, he had awakened on Doodland (as it had been then) and it had been a joyous awakening. He'd had a very happy life there, with lots of new friends who'd welcomed him and made him feel at home. At the time he'd had no idea that someone had created him, or how he'd come into existence. Since then, however, he'd wondered on many an occasion why anyone would want to create a monster like Crevitos and then unleash him on the poor, unsuspecting Creations of Doodland. Anthony had tried to explain that, to his creator, Crevitos was just a cartoon, not a real, living being. But Boff was still bemused: he simply couldn't fathom why anyone would want to create a being so vicious and evil and cruel…*

At some point, Saddler had either slid or half woken and settled himself into a lying down position on the slab.

It was something scuttling across his face that woke Saddler up and he shot, confused, into an upright position. His lantern was flickering in a desultory way that suggested it might just give up the ghost at any moment. The thought of being stranded in complete pitch darkness in this labyrinth of passages, galvanized Saddler into action. Groaning with the stiffness that seemed to have crept into every one of his bones as he slept on the hard, cold wedge of rock, Saddler located his backpack in the gloom and searched in it for a new candle and some matches.

Carefully, so as not to drip any wax on the waning flame of the existing candle, Saddler held the new wick to the flame until it caught. Then he pushed the bottom of the new candle securely on top of the old, holding it there for a moment until it cooled slightly. Now the new candle was held firmly in place by the pooled wax of the old. Saddler closed the lantern door gently, so as not to risk creating a draft that would extinguish the fledgling flame. The matches he returned to his back-pack unused; hopefully his journey wouldn't be too long, but best not to be wasteful.

As it strengthened, the flame revived Saddler's spirits a little, and he delved into his backpack again for a slice of sugarloaf and a few sips of nut juice to refresh his dry throat and mouth.

There was absolutely no way of knowing how long he'd slept; it could have been five minutes, or five hours. Certainly, nearer the latter he was sure, since he now felt quite rested. The sugarloaf and nut juice soon worked their magic and he felt much more optimistic about continuing his journey.

Taking the map Ting had given him from his pocket, Saddler unfolded it and held the lantern close to shine a better light on the complex web of tunnels that criss-crossed this remote part of the mine. The path he was on was clearly marked and, provided he didn't stray from it, would lead him without too many twists and turns to the outer edge of the mine. The exit, Ting had told him, was well disguised among several deep crevices in the mountainous terrain upon which Crevitos's castle stood.

It all seemed fairly straightforward so, now that he felt rested, he thought he'd better not waste any more time.

As if to make the point, something scurried across Saddler's hand, where it now rested with the map on the stone slab. Saddler snatched his hand away hurriedly, catching just the briefest glimpse of a small shadowy form with what seemed like a whole host of nasty, tickly legs.

"Yep, time you was 'eading out!" Saddler told himself in the stillness, trying to erase from his mind the thought that some similar spectral creature had crawled across his face earlier.

He folded the map once more and tucked it safely into his jacket pocket. Hoisting his backpack onto his shoulders, he picked up his lamp and stepped out once more onto the rough-hewn path. He hadn't gone much farther, when the path began to climb slightly as Ting had told him it would. From the map, Saddler knew that he would soon come upon a T junction at which he needed to make a right-hand turn and, not too much longer after that, a left-hand turn would take him up and out of the mine. With any luck, it wouldn't be much more than another hour or so before he would finally reach the exit.

Sure enough, before he had gone too much further, Saddler found himself standing at the T junction. He lifted his lantern high and made a right turn; it took a huge effort of will not to hurry now that he was so close to his goal.

It was just as well he didn't rush. Unaccountably, ahead of him the darkness seemed (though surely this wasn't possible) even darker. Beyond his lamp, the tunnel was pitch black anyway, so how could it be any blacker?

A sense of sickening foreboding washed over him as he inched his way more cautiously forwards.

And came up against a solid wall of rock.

The tunnel had collapsed.

Taking deep breaths to steady his rising panic, Saddler held his lantern aloft and checked over every inch of the rock-fall. Could he perhaps shift enough debris to find just the smallest way through? Finding a couple of loose rocks, he pulled them away, scrabbling at the ones behind them until a shower of stones and rubble from above brought him to his senses.

It was no use.

The path was blocked.

Overcome with despair, Saddler sank to his knees and buried his head in his hands; the candlelight could not begin to pierce the gloom that now settled around him.

# CHAPTER FORTY-THREE
# SMALL THINGS

*Nyctophobia - also known as fear of the dark.*

*Whether this phobia is something that can affect other creatures than humans isn't widely known. On Earth, it's considered to be quite a normal part of growing up for children between about 6 and 12, but it wasn't something Saddler could honestly say he'd come across before his journey through the mines of Doomland. After some discussion with the Prof, Saddler felt only slightly reassured that his own ensuing fear of the dark would resolve itself, since it was caused by the specific trauma of being in the mines. Remove the trauma and the fear would hopefully sort itself out - over time…*

Something touched Saddler's hand lightly and he jerked his head up violently. Normally a very steady and placid character, he did not know why the thought of these things with multiple legs filled him with such disgust. They were probably just spiders and he wasn't afraid of those. At least on Emajen he wasn't: spiders were friendly, respectful creatures there.

He snatched up his lantern and swung it round rather less cautiously than he should. The flame wavered alarmingly, reminding him that he really didn't want to end up surrounded by this sinister blackness with no light at all, especially if there were nasty crawly things lurking amongst the shadows.

Saddler's knees were sore from kneeling on the craggy ground and he set his lantern down to steady himself against the wall of fallen rock. Groaning, he pulled himself stiffly upright. As he did so, he caught just the very hint of movement to his side, behind one of the large boulders wedged there.

"Oo's there?"

Nothing.

"Don't make me come and find ya!" Saddler managed to sound a great deal sterner than he felt. Truthfully, his heart was thumping so hard, he thought it might easily cause another rock fall.

But he was rewarded by the sight of a small head that peered warily around the side of the boulder. Whatever it was, he figured that it was at least as scared of him as he was of it. His heartbeat began to subside a little and his shoulders peeled themselves away from his ears.

"I won't 'urt ya," Saddler said less gruffly this time.

A pair of shoulders joined the small head. Extraordinarily large round eyes blinked nervously and surveyed Saddler uncertainly.

Saddler thought for a moment, then slowly, so as not to scare the creature, he bent down and felt in his backpack for a small piece of sugarloaf. It was the only thing he could think of that might tempt the creature to come a bit nearer.

He held the sugarloaf in his outstretched hand and waited patiently. He could see the small being's soft, furry little snout twitch, as the sweet, heady scent reached its nostrils. Before Saddler could react, it had whipped from behind the boulder, snatched the piece of sugarloaf from his hand and disappeared behind the rock again. Rather satisfying munching sounds ensued. Even in the circumstances, Saddler couldn't help but smile.

He dug in his backpack and broke off another small piece. This time, he held on to it more tightly. The small head and shoulders appeared again.

"Hmm, nice, was it? Want some more, do ya?" Slowly, Saddler lowered himself to the floor once more and settled himself as comfortably as was possible. Just at this very moment, he wasn't going anywhere. There were a number of options all jostling for space in his head, but only one that he knew, in his heart of hearts, would be the necessary choice. It was not going to be an easy decision and he was not quite ready to make it yet.

So, he sat quietly and patiently, morsel in hand, waiting for the sugarloaf to win out over fear.

It took a while. There were a few cautious attempts by the little creature to approach Saddler, and several mad dashes back to the safety of the boulder.

However, once tasted, the sugarloaf was a powerful draw.

Finally, Saddler's patience was rewarded and before too long, the little creature was nestled comfortably on his lap, contentedly nibbling away and making surprisingly loud smacking noises for one so small. Saddler stroked it gently and soothingly and they sat together this way for some while.

# CHAPTER FORTY-FOUR
# OPTIONS

*Whilst Anthony and Destiny had become quite used to travelling to Emajen from Earth and back again, it still never ceased to amaze them that time itself was very different in both places. For example, it could be night time on Earth and day time on Emajen. Likewise it could be winter in one place, yet spring in the other. Alternatively, time or season could be the same in both. It was an odd thing to try to get your head around. Time could go faster on Emajen, but it could also go slower. Whatever it was doing at the moment, it seemed that it was only a few months since their epic journey and the Battle of Emajen, whichever world you were on. Strange…*

It was a beautiful day on Emajen. The Prof and Saddler had wrestled with Nebiré's great wicker chair and had finally managed to manoeuvre it down the long corridor and out onto the grass.

Everyone had been horrified by the turn of events in the mines. Saddler was an extraordinary story teller: his listeners found themselves transported to the very time and place he was revisiting. They shared his every emotion, as though they were all reliving his experiences.

Now, outside Nebiré's abode, surrounded by the sweet smells of spring, cheerful birdsong and the gentle rustle of trees stretching and yawning and slowly awakening from their long winter slumber, it was almost impossible to imagine being stuck in the dark, fetid extremity of Doomland's mines.

***

Back on Earth, between visits to listen to Saddler's unfolding story, Destiny and Anthony had discussed at length what Saddler's options in the mines would be.

"Well, he could stay where he was and hope someone would rescue him," Destiny had said thoughtfully.

"Why would they even look for him, though?" Anthony had countered. "As far as Ting and his friends were concerned, they couldn't actually know whether Saddler had succeeded or not."

"No, that's true. Maybe his little friend could have been sent to get help?"

"Well, until we see Saddler again, we won't know if it was just a random little creature, or something that could actually help him," Anthony mused.

"Dodgy, anyway," Destiny had said firmly. "I think staying put would be giving up, and I can only think of one ending to that!"

"I think you're right. So, another option would be to retrace his steps, find Ting and try to work out another way to escape," said Anthony.

"That would mean getting past all the guards and an extremely angry Snake!"

"It would. Plus, as far as we know, the Creations hadn't found any other way out of the mines, so he would have to get back up into the castle and out that way, without being seen."

"And supposing Crevitos had got back by then?" Destiny had shuddered at the thought.

"They would be on high alert all over the place. No, there's no way he could even attempt it."

There had been a short silence, while they both digested this thought. Then Destiny said, "I suppose he could have used the gateway Nebiré gave him. She didn't say it definitely wouldn't work in the mines. Only that she wasn't sure it would be strong enough."

"Yes," said Anthony. "But that's as much of a long shot as waiting and hoping against hope that someone might rescue you. And if it didn't work, what then? Saddler would be stranded on Doomland for good."

They looked at each other as the significance of the choice that remained for Saddler hovered unsaid between them. Finally, Destiny said slowly: "So that only leaves one option…"

"The third route!" Anthony finished for her.

***

Now, seated around Nebiré on the grass, with Kaz munching contentedly nearby, Destiny could understand why Saddler had suggested that they sit outside on this bright, calm spring day, to continue the story.

# CHAPTER FORTY-FIVE
# DARKNESS AND LIGHT

*Emajen and Doodland – two worlds where inhabitants lived contentedly together and meanness was a very rare thing. It was unbelievably sad that two such calm and lovely worlds could have been so devastated by a character created by a human being on Earth. Anthony and Destiny were thankful they'd been able to help those worlds, but wished it hadn't been someone from their own who'd caused so much trouble in the first place…*

There was a strange serenity to sitting here in the semi-dark, with the odd, furry little creature on his lap. Saddler's eyelids began to droop. Thoughts scattered across his brain like tumbleweed, tired and battered as his brain was from all the traumatic experiences Crevitos had bombarded it with. Would it really be so bad, was one thought, to just sit here peacefully and quietly with his little companion? Now that he wasn't alone, his panic had melted away like fragile snow. What could he really do anyway? Even if he made it back to Emajen, where would he even begin with trying to defeat someone as powerful as Crevitos?

A couple of times, he jerked his eyes open wide as another part of his brain tried valiantly to battle against such negative thoughts. Finally, his eyes closed; the lids felt heavy with a debilitating lethargy that Saddler felt helpless to grapple with.

He was sliding, not fast, but insistently into a dark abyss. And it was almost a relief…

There was a light touch on his hand. It felt familiar but was not enough to really rouse him. The pull of the darkness was too strong.

There it was again. And again. A flicker of annoyance disturbed Saddler's lassitude.

The touch became more demanding. Saddler's descent faltered. A moment elapsed, where he teetered on the edge of the abyss. The darkness seemed so soothing after so many struggles.

Then he felt a sharp pain, which brought him rushing back up towards the light of consciousness.

His eyes sprang open. In the wavering candlelight, he saw that his hand was bleeding.

Everything came flooding back and although his situation was dire in the extreme, he couldn't believe he had almost given in – almost given up.

He glanced around for his little friend, who was no longer on his lap. Scared, round eyes peered from behind the boulder once more.

"I wouldn't ordinarily fank someone for bitin' me," Saddler said gently, "But I fink I might just owe you my life little one!"

The creature looked cautiously at Saddler: it seemed to make up its mind that he really wasn't cross. Like a small streak of lightning, it sped across the rocky ground and up Saddler's arm, onto his shoulder, where it proceeded to lick his cheek and nibble his ear as if to say sorry.

"Alright, alright!" Saddler found himself laughing. It felt strange; it was something he didn't seem to have done in a very long time. But it also felt good. It was as if the laughter had awoken something in his brain that had been locked away for too long.

He put his hand up to pet the animal and was astounded when it began to gently lick his wound. He watched, fascinated, as the tiny pink tongue gently worked its way around the edges of the small nip, cleaning it and soothing away the slight stinging sensation Saddler had felt. Once it had stopped, the creature looked at Saddler with large, expectant eyes and, what he was convinced was a small smile.

Saddler lowered his big hand. He peered at it closely. He looked at his small friend and back at his hand.

"Well, that's 'andy, so to speak. Fank you again little one." Saddler received a nibble on the ear by way of reply. He looked at his hand once more. There was not the slightest sign that there had ever been a wound there.

Giving his companion one final pat, Saddler gently lowered it to the floor. Bending down, Saddler said seriously: "I don't know 'ow to fank you enough, and I 'ate to leave you 'ere, but I guess this is your 'ome. I 'ave to go back. I 'ave to go back to the only way that's left for me to go."

Saddler could have sworn that the little creature's face fell. This felt like one of the hardest things he had ever had to do. Shouldering his backpack, he took two steps forward, then turned back.

Unless…" he said. With an unmistakeable squeak of joy, the tiny creature scampered up his trouser leg and up his sleeve, onto his shoulder once more.

"…you cared to come wiv me!" Saddler laughed again as he finished his sentence.

"I don't even know if you 'ave a name," Saddler said. An answering squeak sounded remarkably like 'Nub'.

"Nub?"

Was that really a nod of the head?

"That's your name? Nub?"

Saddler watched closely. There! A definite nod, he was sure of it.

"Nub it is then. Well, Nub I 'ave no idea what we're gonna find, but since we 'ave no other choice, we'd better get going. I'll be really glad of your company 'owever far you want to come.

But if fings get 'airy, you scarper, OK? I don't want anyfing 'appening to you. You 'ear me?"

Nub snuggled into Saddler's cheek but didn't make any sign of hearing or understanding what Saddler had just said.

"Hmmm, seems you've got selective 'earing. I know a quave at 'ome a bit like you! Well, if we do make it out of 'ere and back to Emajen, and if we do defeat Crevitos (and that's a lot of big 'ifs') I'll make sure you 'ave as much sugarloaf as it's possible for such a tiny mite as yourself to eat!"

So saying, Saddler began to retrace his steps through the mine.

# CHAPTER FORTY-SIX
# INSEPARABLE

*The first time the Prof had seen a Creation was when Boff had found his way out of the mines and had been discovered hiding in a bush by Squib. Lots of Creations, Boff included, are very human-like, and Boff could fairly easily have passed for an inhabitant of Emajen, perhaps just from a part of that world that Saddler hadn't yet come across. Many Creations though, and Boff was one of them, have a slightly cartoony look about them. On Crevitos, it wasn't very noticeable unless you looked really closely...*

Whether it was having company, or just a new feeling of resolve, Saddler found that retracing his steps seemed to take far less time than the opposite journey had.

At times, Nub rode contentedly on Saddler's shoulder; at others she would scamper down to the ground, disappear for a short while and then return to Saddler's shoulder once more. Saddler had an idea that perhaps Nub was scouting ahead, checking for signs of danger. Whether that was true or not, they reached the alcove he had rested in before without any mishap.

This time, they stopped only for a brief moment or two, just to catch their breath - or at least, Saddler's breath. He also needed to take a second to prepare himself for the next part of the journey. It probably wouldn't take too long now to get back to the intersection where the path branched three ways.

From this direction, the right-hand path would take him back up to the working part of the mine. Straight ahead would be the path Ting had told him was impassibly blocked. So, he would have to take what was now the path to his left.

The path where untold dangers lay. The path he had been warned at all costs to avoid. The path he now had no option but to follow.

Saddler straightened his back and lifted his chin. Whatever happened from now on, at least he would know he had given it his best shot.

"Time to make a move," he said firmly, more to himself than Nub.

Nub stroked Saddler's cheek with a gentle paw, almost as though she knew how Saddler was feeling.

"I'm not so 'appy about you coming any further." Saddler had carefully placed Nub on his hand. Nub was so small that she nestled comfortably in Saddler's palm. She tilted her head slightly and regarded him with large baleful eyes.

"Now that ain't fair." Saddler attempted to joke, even though his stomach was beginning to knot itself most uncomfortably.

"If Ting was right (and I've no reason to believe 'e's not) there's no telling what we might meet on the next path. You can look at me now wiv those big, sad eyes, but I just don't want anyfing to 'appen to you!"

Nub chattered at him in the shrill little voice he was now becoming very accustomed to. He had no idea what she was saying, but when she scurried up his arm and back into her place on his shoulder, it seemed obvious enough that she had made up her mind.

He stroked her affectionately and bent to retrieve the lamp from the slab. He had inserted a new candle into the lamp; there were now only two replacement candles left. They had better hope that the next leg of their journey didn't last too long.

# CHAPTER FORTY-SEVEN
# THE PATH OF DOOM

*Most Creations are by nature gently, friendly souls, unless they have been created with a particular purpose in mind that is. When Anthony, Destiny and Saddler first encountered a group of Creations, it was on Emajen. The group had been rescued from the mines by Boff and had managed to build a small community in some underground caves. At that time, it was understandable that those Creations were wary of any other beings than themselves. Having narrowly escaped Crevitos's tyranny on one world they quite naturally didn't want to risk becoming prey to some despot on another. Anthony, Destiny and Saddler had stumbled on their hiding place and been incarcerated whilst the Creations decided what to do about them. It was where all three had encountered Boff, and it was only the first of several times that Creations had come to one or other of the trio's aid…*

So here they were at the convergence of the paths. All three radiated the same stifling, black nothingness as they had the first time Saddler had stood at this point.

He knew it couldn't really be so, but the path to his left seemed to throb with a dark malevolent intelligence that he had not noticed before.

"Well," he said resolutely, "no point just standing 'ere. Best foot forward and all that!" He was rewarded by an encouraging head-butt from Nub. It occurred to Saddler that yet again, here was someone who was prepared to help him even though there was no reason why she should - just as Anthony and Destiny had done.

"This might turn out to be the most expensive bit of sugar loaf you've ever 'ad," Saddler remarked grimly. Nonetheless, the tiny presence of Nub gave rise to a small flicker of hope in Saddler's heart.

"Right-o then!" This time, his voice was brisk. With a deliberate sense of purpose, Saddler stepped forward on to the path of doom.

It was not his imagination. A few steps along the path, the air around them altered noticeably. It was thick - you could almost touch it. It was fetid and it pulsated, as though it were a living, breathing organism in its own right.

Nub had deserted her perch on Saddler's shoulder and found an inside pocket in his jacket where he could feel her nestling against his heart. Saddler kept up a flow of soothing chatter, (not that there was really much to talk about down here) as much for his own sanity as to reassure Nub. They hadn't gone far at all when the path began to dip very steeply downwards. A far sharper descent than there had been the other way. Saddler's lantern struggled to illuminate the viscous blackness and he soon lost track of the time and distance once more.

In places, the downward slope was so steep that Saddler had to steady himself with one hand against the rough-hewn wall of the tunnel. Soon he ceased talking and fumbled his way in silence, saving all his energy to concentrate on placing one foot in front of the other.

Nub too was so still that soon it felt as though Saddler were once more walking alone through a pitch-black nightmare - one that seemed to have no end.

Then, without warning, Saddler walked smack into a solid wall. For a moment, he stood rubbing his forehead, stunned rather than hurt, rudely shocked out of his almost trance-like state.

"Not again!"

Surely after all this, the path of doom wasn't blocked too?

Saddler felt Nub stir within his pocket. By now he had become quite accustomed to the way she scampered up and down.

"You OK, Nub?" he queried.

For a few seconds there was no reply. Then Saddler heard a slight scrabbling behind him. The next moment, Nub had appeared with Ting's map in her tiny paws. Once again, Saddler was amazed at her ability to make him laugh - even in the grimmest of circumstances. Now, looking at this tiny creature struggling with the map, that was three times her size even though it was folded, Saddler couldn't help but chuckle.

"You're a treasure!" Fondly, he tickled Nub under her chin and relieved her of the cumbersome map. It was difficult to see by the candlelight, but with Nub's help, Saddler managed to locate the path they were on.

"'Ow is it you can follow a map?" Saddler was astonished. This little soul had no end of talents. It wasn't a question Nub could easily answer, but Saddler began to wonder whether she had always lived in these dark, forbidding passages, or whether she had merely escaped here to hide from Crevitos and his cronies.

It didn't take long for Saddler to realize his mistake. Well, actually, two mistakes. Number one, he should have checked the map out before he embarked on this path, and, two, he should have followed the path to his right. It had divided at a fork, not very far back from where they now stood. This one was clearly a dead end.

Saddler folded the map once more. This time, he tucked it in his jacket pocket so that he could reach it more easily.

Now he knew that he needed to keep to the left of this path and retrace his steps until they came to where it split. After that, it looked like there were a number of twists and turns so he would need to check the map frequently to avoid getting lost in this maze of tunnels.

Yet another detour, but he only had himself to blame. He needed to keep his wits about him and be much more vigilant from here on. The mines appeared to have a sneaky way of sliding into your brain and making you dull and careless. Well now he had realized what was happening, he would strive hard to stay alert at all times. Danger number one: not what he had been expecting, but one he had very nearly fallen for. In some ways it was just as well he'd come up against a dead end and not ended up wandering aimlessly through the warren of passages until he was hopelessly lost.

Not just he - they! He had a responsibility to look after Nub too, although, so far it had been rather more the other way around.

Nub was back in his inside pocket, so Saddler gave her a careful pat.

"'Ere we go again," he said and he was heartened by a muffled squeak by way of reply.

# CHAPTER FORTY-EIGHT
# A STICKY SITUATION

*As Saddler recounted his journey through the mines, Anthony found himself thinking back to the time on their quest that Saddler had disappeared. Anthony, Destiny and Boff had all been tricked into drinking what had seemed like a perfectly innocuous beverage, which had knocked them out cold, not to mention giving them severe hallucinations. It had all been part of Crevitos's efforts to stop them finding the Natorqua. The after effects had left them feeling woozy and out of sorts, which was why Saddler had left them to go in search of provisions for the rest of their journey. He should have only been gone for a few hours. When he hadn't returned the next day, they had all decided they must continue the quest without him. Naturally, they'd been worried, but Anthony thought that even in their wildest dreams none of them could have guessed the horrors Saddler would have to endure...*

For a while all went smoothly. Having corrected their path, Saddler kept a close eye on the map, stopping to check it at frequent intervals. He tried to make these stops as brief as possible, for two reasons: one he was trying to conserve the candles, and two he was beginning to wonder what might be happening up on Doomland way above. He had no way of knowing how long this journey had taken him so far, but it felt too long - far too long. For all he knew, Crevitos might have already returned. He could have sent out a search party and that didn't bear thinking about. Saddler could hardly run away. He wouldn't know where he was going. No, on both counts, moving forward as steadily as possible was really the only option. Saddler realized with a jolt that he was getting lost in his thoughts once more. Hurriedly, he checked the map to reassure himself that they were still on the right track. Satisfied that he hadn't missed any vital turns, he continued on as quickly as he dared. The path had levelled a little now, which made the going slightly easier. Saddler was just beginning to wonder whether he should have followed this route in the first place, when he trod on something that stopped him dead.

"Oh, gross," he muttered, assuming it must be an unpleasant package some animal had left lying around. He would just have to hope that he would be able to clean his boot at some point.

Stepping forward again, Saddler felt his other foot sliding on something soft and squishy, something that made a most revolting squelching sound. He attempted to lift his right foot and discovered that whatever it was he had trodden in, was sticking to his boot like glue. He had to steady himself against the wall of the tunnel to extricate one foot after the other, so that he could step back a couple of paces onto dry ground.

Bending low, Saddler held his lantern close to the floor. Something glistened stickily. Saddler picked up a small piece of rock and dipped it experimentally in the gloopy substance. As he tried to pull it free, treacly strands like viscous spittle dripped from the stone, reluctant to let it go.

"What on Emajen…?"

But of course, he wasn't on Emajen! And there was absolutely no way of knowing what had produced or created this. There was also no way of knowing how far it extended. Saddler found another piece of rock and weighed it thoughtfully in his hand. Then he threw it as hard as he could in front of him. It landed with a soft squelch some way down the passage.

"Rats!" Saddler exclaimed. "Not just a few steps of the stuff then." He bent close to the floor once more, examining the edges. Nub appeared on his shoulder and squeaked at him enquiringly. Saddler explained. Then he said: "But just as I thought, look 'ere, along the edges it ain't too bad. Gonna slow us down a bit, but I've checked the map and it ain't too far to the next stop. 'Opefully, whatever it is, won't be down there too."

Nub snuggled into his neck as Saddler blew out his lamp and hung it carefully on his belt. He would need both hands to steady his way along the edge of the path, but he would be able to feel as soon as they reached the opening to the next passage they needed to turn down.

It was only seconds later that they heard the noise.

It was a dragging, slurping sort of sound, as though something heavy was sliding steadfastly through the goo.

"I dunno what made this mess, but I fink we're just about to find out!"

Round the bend in the tunnel, a strange, pale glow preceded the eerie dragging sound. The glow lit the tunnel with a cold, menacing light. Nub quivered on Saddler's shoulder, as Saddler stood transfixed. There was nothing he could do. Whatever it was, was approaching fast. There was no way he would be able to retrace his steps through the glutenous mess, quick enough to escape. Behind the light, emerged a shape. It was huge and bulbous; it near enough filled the whole tunnel.

Saddler cupped his hand protectively around Nub, who still trembled miserably on his shoulder.

"I'm so sorry," Saddler whispered softly, "You should never 'ave come!"

# CHAPTER FORTY-NINE
# A STICKY END

*Despite everyone's reassurances that Saddler had nothing to feel guilty about, it would be a long, long time (perhaps never) before he didn't blame himself for – as he saw it – letting everyone down. One of the things he blamed himself for most was leading Nub into the most awful, frightening and dangerous situations. He berated himself for not just leaving her where he'd found her in the mines, even though he knew she had been most insistent about staying with him. But then, the thought of her alone in that dark, forbidding place was also too much to bear. Sometimes it was all just too hard for him to get his head around…*

The situation was surreal, like being in a dream you couldn't run away from. The light, the noise and the blob approached relentlessly. Saddler let go of Nub and searched frantically in his pockets for something to defend himself with. There was a knife in his backpack, but there was no time. All his fingers alighted on was a sharp pencil. Maybe he could stab it in the creature's eye - if it had an eye; at this juncture, it was almost impossible to tell. It was merely an amorphous blob (a vast one at that) with no discernible features at all.

Within moments, the creature was upon them. Its foul odour made Saddler retch, as it stopped bare inches from where he stood. No eyes that could be seen! That was that plan out of the window, then, and he didn't readily have another to mind.

The freakish light around the blob, seemed to throb as various parts of its anatomy bulged and then retracted with a series of moist slobbering thwacks. It could hardly have been more than a second, but it felt like an age to Saddler, as he gazed, stupefied and repulsed at the creature before him.

Then, without warning, a hole opened in the gruesome beast's quivering flesh. The edges of the aperture puckered and rippled and the stench that gushed from that vile orifice was truly nauseating.

Saddler opened his mouth to yell a warning to Nub, but as he did so, there was a sickening rush of air as the blob sucked in the very atmosphere around it. Helplessly, Saddler watched, horrified, as Nub was torn from his shoulder. Nub's tiny body flailed helplessly in the great gush of wind that sucked her inevitably towards the gaping hole.

In an instant, she was gone.

"Noo!" Saddler shrieked with despair. Oblivious, the creature now closed the small gap between them. Saddler found himself pinned against the rough-hewn tunnel wall. Foul, sticky blubber filled his eyes, nose and mouth, suffocating him. He had only moments before it would be all over. Barely aware of what he was doing, Saddler clasped his fist firmly around the pencil he still held in his hand. It was, no doubt, a vain gesture, but it was all he had.

With the little strength he had in his now oxygen starved body, Saddler plunged the pencil as deep as he could into the great pulsating blob in front of him.

There was a nano-second's pause before the seething mass exploded like a vast balloon. The sound reverberated off the walls of the tunnel and Saddler was momentarily deafened by the boom. It was immediately followed by a deluge of glutenous gloop that rained down on him from all directions. He was dripping from head to foot with the noxious substance, but he was alive.

"NUB!" Saddler fell to his knees, anguished. He barely heard the tiny, trembling squeak that came from amongst the pool of viscous goo. Then it came again, and Saddler's heart leapt with joy.

"Nub, where are you?" Frantically, he scanned the debris, which still produced a sticky glow, although it was fading rapidly. Finally, he spied a small, dark blob and lunged forward to grasp Nub out of the vile mess. Viscous strands clung to Nub as though disinclined to release her, but Saddler tugged hard until they reluctantly gave way. For several minutes, he held Nub to him until her trembling began to subside. Then, by the light of the fading glow around them, he picked his way along the passage until he reached the turning. With a feeling of relief, he stepped out of the goo onto dry ground. As he did so, he heard another sound, a welcome one this time; the sound of running water.

# CHAPTER FIFTY
# A MATTER OF LIFE AND DEATH

*Of all the assembled company, it was perhaps Boff who could most closely empathise with Saddler's desperate attempts to escape Doomland. Crevitos was a formidable enemy, and once Saddler had committed himself to leave, Crevitos would know that Saddler was no longer under his control. There were many, many terrible things about Crevitos, but in Boff's view the worst thing was that extraordinarily beautiful face. A face that could mock, or sneer, or portray demonic cruelty and yet the very fact of its beauty made those things so very much worse. It made Boff shudder just to think of it…*

Poor Nub was trembling with both cold and fear. Saddler had tried hard to remove as much of the slimy gloop as possible, but her fur was drenched and matted with the stuff.

And there was another problem too. Saddler's lantern had also been saturated in the substance and the current candle was useless. He had hoped that a little warmth from the flame might help to warm Nub up. Instead, all he could think of was to tuck her back into his inside pocket once more.

The sound of running water was quite loud - it couldn't be too far. Saddler thought it best to feel his way along the passage wall towards the sound. If the water seemed fresh, he could replenish his water bottle and set about cleaning his lantern so he could light a new candle.

He had not gone very far at all when he felt his way around a bend in the tunnel wall. Immediately, the sound intensified: flaming torches were dotted around the far side of what he could now see was a wide pool. At one end of this, a small waterfall created a series of bubbles and ripples that sparkled and shimmered in the torch light. Saddler stopped in his tracks and surveyed the scene warily. Burning torches meant company. Whether that company was friendly or hostile, he had no way of knowing. It was Nub shivering in his inner pocket that made Saddler's mind up for him. All the while she was covered in goo, she appeared to be getting colder. As he plucked her gently from inside his coat, he realised that the stuff wasn't drying at all on her matted fur. There was simply no option. He needed to get her cleaned up and dried - otherwise she could die There was no sign of life at the moment, anywhere around the cave. With any luck (and they could definitely do with some of that) they could be cleaned up and on their way before whoever, or whatever, had lit these torches appeared.

Gently, Saddler cupped Nub in his hand and held her close to his chest. Cautiously, he made his way around the edge of the water to where the waterfall gushed into the pool below. Nub trembled fitfully in his hand, although she seemed to have fallen into a troubled doze. There was no time to waste - he couldn't afford to be too gentle.

"Sorry, little mate," he said softly, before plunging Nub unceremoniously under the steady flow of water. It was cold enough to make him gasp and he hurriedly rubbed at the stickiness on Nub with his other hand, but he daren't keep her under this icy flow for too long. However, Nub didn't seem to be aware of what was happening to her; she didn't even open her eyes. Hurriedly, Saddler pulled her out again. Was it too late? Had the bitter chill of the waterfall been too much for her? Saddler fought to keep calm. There was no time for him to panic. Ignoring the cold, he shrugged off his jacket and quickly removed the woollen jumper he was wearing. Nub was so small the garment totally engulfed her. Saddler wrapped her up snugly and made his way over to the nearest torch. It was set quite high on the wall of the cavern, so he gently set her down and lifted the torch from its bracket. To one side, there was a group of rocks that would make a good resting place for the torch. With a brief, worried glance at Nub, Saddler hastened to the rocks to lodge the flaming torch securely so that he would be able to use both hands to dry Nub by the heat of the flames.

"Just don't let me be too late," he muttered fearfully. Without his jumper and jacket, the cold was beginning to seep into his bones. Saddler shivered. Time enough though, to worry about his needs. Nub was all that mattered right now.

"Hang on little one." Saddler hurried back to the spot where Nub lay wrapped in his jumper.

Except she wasn't there!

Saddler cast around him feverishly. This was the right spot; he knew it was, yet still he searched frantically about him in case he'd got it wrong.

Finally, he stopped and stared helplessly at the water.

He hadn't got it wrong! He had, for the very best of reasons, left Nub alone in this hellish place for mere seconds. Now she was gone!

As he stared disconsolately into the glassy depths of the pool, Saddler felt a sharp sting to his neck.

By the time his brain had registered the sensation, his legs had crumpled beneath him and Saddler lay in a heap, oblivious to everything, on the unforgiving cavern floor.

# CHAPTER FIFTY-ONE
# CONFUSED

*Magic – a dictionary definition of this would be something along the lines of influencing things or events using supernatural forces. It could be said that the definition of magic may well vary from place to place and time to time. Certainly, many of the things that happen on Emajen might very well be construed as magical to human beings on Earth – just the fact of travel between worlds is not something most humans would consider normal. For Destiny and Anthony, their time on Emajen could at the very least be described as life changing. Earth wasn't somewhere your average 21st century person expected to find magic. Or was it? Maybe human beings just need to look a little closer…*

Saddler opened his eyes and groaned. Every part of him seemed to ache from head to foot and his head thumped dully as though he'd smacked it on something hard.

For a moment or two, he struggled to become fully conscious. He was transported to another time and place when he had awoken in a bed in a circular, gloomy room, rather like this one, with a very similar, banging headache. Just for a second, he thought he was in the same place again. His heart sank at the thought that he'd been recaptured and was back right where he'd started.

Then, as his eyes accustomed themselves to the gloom, he realized that this place was, in fact, very different. To begin with, it was actually a small cave, and although there was a stout wooden door at the entrance, it was slightly ajar as if to reassure him that he was not a prisoner here.

The light in the cave came not only from the burning torches on the walls, which actually gave off quite a cheery glow, but also from a brazier which burned steadily and emitted a welcome warmth.

Whatever it was that Saddler was resting on, had been heaped with blankets and cushions. It was so warm and comfortable that, despite his best efforts, Saddler slipped into a restful doze again.

The next time he awoke, although his head still ached, he felt more alert. Gingerly, he attempted to push himself up into a sitting position. The next thing he knew, something had launched itself at him, and before he could react, he was being licked and head-butted all over his face.

"Woah, woah, steady on!" Instantly, all else was forgotten, as Saddler sat Nub on his hand and gazed at her with a mixture of joy and amazement.

Her fur was clean and dry, her eyes were bright and she nibbled his fingers gently to show that she was overjoyed to see that Saddler was alive and well.

"How…?" he began to ask, just as a scruffy dog-like creature trotted through the door.

"Oh good, oh good," it said. "At last you're awake! I see too, that you have been reunited with your little friend. Good! Good!" Its voice was gruff, but the words were kind. Saddler relaxed. Whoever this was, there had been plenty of time for it to get rid of him if that had been what it wanted.

"I believe I 'ave to thank you, and I do so wiv all my 'eart," Saddler said gravely. He looked at Nub and his heart swelled with joy at how well she looked.

"Ah, yes, well, glad to be of service and all that. My name is Herbert, by the way."

"Saddler. And this is Nub."

"I think you might have forgotten the apology bit, Herbert." This comment was made by a new creature that had just entered the cave. It was, indeed, one of the most beautiful quaves Saddler had ever set eyes on. Its fur was long and looked sumptuously soft; in the torchlight, shades of gold and amber shimmered and danced as the creature moved. Deep golden eyes regarded them curiously. Saddler had never come across a quave that wasn't curious, and he was sure Destiny had told him that cats on Earth were much the same. Its gaze was kind, but with just a hint of wariness.

"Indeed, I was just getting to that bit." Herbert gave the newcomer the sort of look that suggested perhaps they had been the best of friends for a long time.

"As Champers here has so kindly reminded me, we do have a bit of an apology to offer." Here, Herbert took a deep breath. "But, perhaps if you're feeling up to it, a little light refreshment might be in order. Then I can explain all, and perhaps you, on your part, can tell us what you're doing here."

# CHAPTER FIFTY-TWO
# QUESTIONS AND ANSWERS

*Anyone who knew Destiny at all would tell you that she was completely animal mad. She couldn't abide any kind of cruelty towards animals and was known to be quite outspoken if she saw someone treating an animal in a way they shouldn't. The very first time that she and Anthony had come across Saddler at a horse show in London he had been kicking up a hell of a stink over a rider who'd been whipping his horse. Looking back now, she thought she'd come to trust Saddler because he was, in so many ways, a kindred spirit…*

Destiny yawned and rubbed her eyes. Saddler's tale was completely exhausting. She felt like she had walked every step alongside him.

"Were they like beings from Emajen, or were they Creations?" Squib wanted to know.

"As it turns out," replied Saddler, "They was actually from Emajen."

"Gosh," said Destiny, "How did that happen?"

"To cut a long story short (and believe me 'erbert's version was very long and complicated indeed) they'd got friendly wiv some of the Creations 'iding on Emajen and decided to 'elp out a bit. They'd set up a few of the caves as a sort of pit stop for Creations trying to escape the mines. Every so often, they would come from Emajen and stay a few days. We was just so lucky they 'appened to be there."

"It doesn't make sense to me." Anthony frowned. "Why there? I thought that was the one route Creations wouldn't take to escape. And wouldn't it be an extremely dodgy place for them to stay?"

"Ah!" Saddler's complexion turned slightly pink. "Well it was the best place for stayin' under Crevitos's radar, so to speak. But actually, if I'd 'ad a mind to study the map more carefully, I'd 'ave seen there was a much quicker way of reaching that very same spot."

"So, in fact," summarized the Prof, "They were not too far from the main passageway up to the mines, but enough out of the way to be safe from Crevitos."

"Exactly," said Saddler.

"Given the circumstances, I'm amazed you even kept going. Not to mention, it must have been virtually impossible reading a map properly by candle light." Destiny defended Saddler staunchly. She knew that none of the others thought Saddler was anything less than a hero, but he always blamed himself - and he shouldn't.

"What I want to know," piped up Boff, "is, what your new friends had to apologize for."

"Two fings," now Saddler smiled at the memory.

"First of all, that ghastly blobby fing was created by one of their 'uman friends to 'elp protect them from unwanted visitors."

"Sort of like a guard dog… er, blob," Anthony said.

"Yeah, sort of like that. So, they was sorry we'd got caught by it and 'ad such an 'orrible time."

"It was extremely effective," remarked the Prof. He searched around in his pockets for a pencil and a piece of paper and began to scribble down some notes.

"What was the other thing?" asked Boff.

"Knocking me out with that sleeping draft fing." Saddler rubbed his neck as though he could still feel the sting of the dart now. "And of course, terrifying me by whisking Nub away."

"That's three things!"

"Mm. Well, anyway, in the 'eat of the moment, they didn't know whether I'd kidnapped Nub and if I was dangerous or not. So, they decided to knock me out first and ask questions later."

"They must have realized pretty quickly that you were trying to help Nub," said Destiny.

"I fink so. It was touch and go there for a while, but I managed to get most of the goo off her under the waterfall, so they dried 'er off and got 'er warmed up in the nick of time. Some'ow, they dragged me to the cave and got me sorted, and that's where I woke up."

"Why didn't they tie you up or something?" queried Anthony. "They still didn't know if you were an enemy or not!"

"Apparently, the first fing Nub did, when she'd recovered enough, was rush around looking for me. Then when she found me, it was obvious how worried she was. They figured, if I was an enemy, I probably wouldn't have been trying to save her."

"What happened to Nub?" Squib asked shyly.

"Oh, she's 'ere abouts somewhere." Saddler smiled and patted his pockets. After a second or two, a small whiskery face and two large round eyes, peaked out from one of his jacket pockets.

"Say 'ello, Nub," he said fondly. "These are my very good friends."

Nub chattered for a moment in her little squeaky voice, rubbed her eyes with tiny paws and whisked back out of sight.

"Oh, my goodness…" Destiny was overcome with delight. Have you ever seen anything so gorgeous, so unbelievably cute."

"Only the last time you saw an animal!" laughed Anthony. "You kept that quiet," he said to Saddler.

"Oh, she's wiv me most of the time," Saddler replied airily. "But she's a bit shy, and it's taken a while for 'er to get accustomed to the light, 'aving been down in the mines for so long. She still prefers the dark, mostly, I fink."

"Has she ever seemed like she wanted to go back there?" asked Destiny. "It might not seem very nice to us, but it was her home."

"I did try asking," said Saddler. Then he chuckled again. "She 'id under the cupboard and refused to come out again. It took all Mrs Saddler's powers of persuasion, and a nice bit of cake, to tempt 'er out. I 'ad to promise faithfully never to mention such a fing again."

There was a muffled squeak from within the depths of Saddler's pocket that set everyone laughing.

"Does she like Mrs Saddler?" asked Destiny.

"Nope, more like adores Mrs Saddler, I would say - especially when Mrs Saddler 'as a nice piece of somefing tasty about 'er person."

"I'm so glad Nub has found such a lovely home," Destiny said with huge satisfaction. "I wish all creatures on Earth were as lucky."

"Maybe one day enough 'umans will realize 'ow precious your world and all its in'abitants are, to set it right again. If enough youngsters are like you two, it's not too late."

"Let's hope so!"

There was a moment's silence before the friends settled themselves down comfortably, to follow the next thread in Saddler's tale once more.

# CHAPTER FIFTY-THREE
# PLANS ARE MADE

*The Prof, whose keen mind meant that he was interested and enthusiastic about almost everything, was particularly fascinated by the ability of Crevitos to manipulate circumstances using his mind power. On Emajen, his face had apparently appeared in some clouds, frightening both Destiny and Kaz half to death. He had also somehow invaded Anthony, Destiny and Boff's minds to the point where he'd made them all believe in a town that didn't actually exist. That, the Prof was sure, could only have been achieved with the help of someone on Emajen. So, when Saddler was in the mines why didn't Crevitos know where he was? Perhaps his powers couldn't penetrate beneath the surface of Doomland, or perhaps that world itself was somehow shielding Saddler. It was all very intriguing. How the Prof would love the chance to quiz Crevitos and find out some answers…*

It had been a long discussion, deep in the mines of Doomland: The tale of how and why Saddler had ended up here was extremely complicated. Champers and Herbert knew all about Crevitos of course, but what they didn't know was that Crevitos had designs on Emajen.

"We'd heard rumours about the Natorqua becoming sick and dying, of course," said Herbert.

"And then there was a story about them in the newspaper," said Champers continuing the thought, "But we had no idea Crevitos was in any way connected."

Something that also came as news to Saddler's new friends, was the fact that the main tunnel out was blocked.

"It's only two days since we came that way. We'll have to ask a party of Creations to help us shift it. It really is the safest way out - perhaps you could help." Herbert tilted his head enquiringly and gazed at Saddler with bright black eyes. Champers, however, having arched his back in a satisfying stretch, disagreed.

"Saddler needs to press on," he said languidly, not sounding hurried at all. "It could take a number of days to shift the rock fall, depending on how far it extends." His golden eyes regarded Saddler seriously.

"I've encountered one or two of the hazards this route has to offer," he continued, "and I know where the pitfalls lie. There are also a couple of short cuts I know, that will lessen the journey considerably. I will travel with you, until we reach the final short passageway - it shouldn't take more than half a day."

"I'm much obliged," Saddler said gratefully. It was quite a relief to know that Champers would accompany him.

"Young Nub can stay here with me," Herbert said kindly. "It's warm and safe, and I'll be glad of her company while Champers is gone."

Nub, who had been curled up on Saddler's lap all this while, obviously exhausted from all her adventures, sat bolt upright. She looked indignantly from one to the other before scrambling up Saddler's front and disappearing inside his jacket. From the depths of an inside pocket, they could hear miniature grumblings of dissent.

"Fank you for your very kind offer," Saddler said gravely (though with a twinkle in his eye) but I fink you'll find Nub will be coming wiv us."

"Rather the impression I got too!" Herbert wagged his bushy eyebrows good humouredly to show that he wasn't at all offended.

"There are a few things it would be wise to take with us," said Champers." Then we should be on our way." He barely seemed to move a muscle and yet in no time at all it seemed everything was ready. Saddler shook Herbert's paw.

"I 'ope we shall meet again on Emajen and in rather better circumstances. Come and 'ave tea wiv me and Mrs Saddler. 'Er cakes are to die for."

"I shall look forward to that immensely. Take care, all of you. While you are gone, Champers, I'll rally some help to start on the rock fall."

And so it was, that with Nub in his pocket and Champers leading the way, Saddler began the final leg of his journey through the bowels of Doomland.

# CHAPTER FIFTY-FOUR
# CHAMPERS LEADS THE WAY

*Squib listened wide eyed throughout Saddler's tale. With his bright little brain almost as full of questions as the Prof's, he mentally stored them away for a time when it might be right to ask them. Since coming to live on Emajen with the Prof, Squib's life had been transformed. Already he'd learnt so much, absorbing everything the Prof could teach him like a greedy sponge. He'd lost his parents too young to remember what it was like to have someone care for you, and there were things he'd been through that made him very wary of other people. On Emajen he'd come across only kindness, especially from the Prof, Saddler and Nebiré. Bit by bit his confidence grew, but he knew only too well what effect cruelty could have on someone. With great empathy for one so young, Squib knew it could be a long time before Saddler would feel able to answer all the questions that Squib burned to ask him. One day, perhaps…*

With Champers as their guide, the trio made much quicker headway than Saddler and Nub had done hitherto. Champers had an ingenious invention which he wore on a headband that emitted a soft but effective light, which easily pierced the blackness some distance in front of them. When Saddler had exclaimed: 'That's a jolly useful bit of equipment', Champers had told him it was powered by the sun and would last for a number of hours before it would need repowering.

Sun power was nothing new to Saddler - many, many things on Emajen were powered by the sun, but he hadn't come across this one before. It occurred to him, that here was an invention the Prof would be interested in. He must remember to describe it when he got back to Emajen. If he got back to Emajen.

Saddler knew, too, that there were things on Earth that were powered by their sun, but he had a feeling that there were often things like batteries involved which caused a lot of waste that was difficult to get rid of. Saddler had just come to the end of his train of thought when Champers stopped dead in front of him. Just managing to avoid colliding with Champers, Saddler berated himself for not concentrating yet again. It was something to do with these long passages that made Saddler retreat into his own thoughts.

Champers wasn't a particularly chatty fellow, but he was speaking now. Saddler snapped his mind back into focus to hear what Champers was saying.

"We need to be wary here, you'll see why in a moment."

They edged forwards slowly, only to stop again a few paces on.

"See," Champers said shortly.

Saddler inched ahead to stand beside Champers and couldn't prevent a cry of dismay escaping from his lips.

In front of them yawned a cavernous hole, which spread almost the entire width of the passage. Its depths could only be imagined. The darkness that radiated from it was palpably evil.

Just the thought of stumbling headlong into this enormous abyss made Saddler shudder. And it was powerful too. Saddler could feel himself being drawn towards the edge of the hole as though something wanted him to join it there. Champers was watching him carefully.

"Fight it!" he said. "You have to be strong, Saddler, or it will suck you in."

Something in his voice made Saddler realize that Champers had already fought this battle of wills, perhaps more than once. Once again, he thanked his lucky stars that Champers was there. On his own, even if he'd avoided falling down the hole, would he have been strong enough to resist its evil lure? Saddler wasn't sure.

In his pocket, Nub stirred restlessly. Saddler lifted his chin stubbornly.

"Back off!" He directed this comment firmly to whatever was down there in the black hole.

"I've got business to attend to. You a'int getting me down there, not for nuffin'!"

There was the weirdest sensation inside his head, almost as though sneaky fingers attempting to grab hold of his will had stopped abruptly. The fingers recoiled rapidly, as though they'd been stung, and Saddler almost believed he could see their retreating shadows slinking silently into the gaping chasm below.

Instantly, he felt lighter, his head clearer. Beside him, Champers gave a brief nod of satisfaction.

"Phew!" Saddler shook his head and let out a long breath. "That felt very much too close," he said grimly. Looking at the gaping hole in front of him, he asked: "What do we do now?"

"Now we cross," came the reply that Saddler had really hoped not to hear.

"'ow?"

There didn't seem to be even the smallest sliver of path that would offer them a way across. Champers tilted his head and angled his headlight so that it illuminated the wall.

"We climb," he remarked briefly.

By the light of the torch, Saddler could now see that there were shallow ledges hewn out of the rock, which were staggered to give foot and hand holds along the wall.

"We climb…" Saddler repeated the words faintly, knowing there was no other option, yet, with a slight lack of conviction at his climbing prowess. Nonetheless, he patted his pocket gently until Nub's small head appeared.

"I want you to go with Champers for this bit," he told Nub firmly, before she could stubbornly refuse. "It will make it easier for me, Nub, if I 'aven't got to worry in case I squash you against the rock."

There was a slight pause, during which Nub was clearly considering this, then she leapt lightly from Saddler's jacket onto the back of Champers and held on tightly to his headband.

Without a word, Champers leapt easily onto the first ledge and then, with no effort, from step to step until he was safely on the other side.

"As easy as that then," Saddler muttered to himself. He could just vaguely see the shape of Champers on the other side of the chasm, behind the glow of light which Champers now helpfully aimed at the wall.

"'Ere we go then!"

Saddler grasped the first of the ledges above him and found a foothold on another lower one. He pulled himself cautiously up and found it wasn't as hard as he'd expected. What Saddler hadn't realized was that he wasn't the same being who had set out with Anthony and Destiny on the quest to find the Natorqua all that time ago. He really had no way of telling how long ago that had been, but it felt like years.

All his experiences and hardships had turned him into a fitter, leaner and stronger being than before. Now it surprized him to find that this challenge was not as daunting as it had at first seemed.

Nonetheless, he was determined not to be complacent. This place had a way of luring you into a false sense of security, so he kept up a running commentary with each step across.

"Come on, Saddler, lad, you can do this! A few more to go and you'll be as safe as 'ouses on the other side. Don't look down now. Don't give that nasty 'ole the slightest reason to suck you in."

About half way across, Saddler paused. He could feel the pull of whatever malevolence lurked in the darkness beneath him. He could almost sense the finger-like tendrils creeping their way back up the sheer sides of the chasm, ready to clutch at the slightest wavering of his will. But he staunchly blocked them from his mind and grasped the next ledge. Nearly there. Just one more foothold to go. Sweating more with the mental effort than the physical toil, Saddler placed his foot firmly on the final foothold. As he shifted his weight across, the ledge crumbled. Saddler grasped frantically at the handhold above it, but his fingers, now slick with fear, slid uselessly across its surface and failed to grab hold. With a cry of despair, Saddler flung himself bodily towards the safety of the path. His body connected, but his legs met only nothingness. He could feel the dark tendrils rushing up to meet him now, and he struggled against the weight of his backpack which threatened to tip him down into the abyss.

Time stilled as he balanced precariously suspended between two conflicting futures - this one with Saddler in it and the one without. He could hear Nub's frantic squeaks close by and it spurred him on to try to pull himself up. Then he felt his wrist grasped by something soft, but unbelievably strong and he realized that Champers was using his tail as a chord to drag him forwards. With a final, gargantuan effort, they heaved together. Saddler was certain he felt the tips of those creepy fingers touch his ankles, as he rolled desperately over the rim of the chasm and lay panting on the tunnel floor.

# CHAPTER FIFTY-FIVE
# ONSLAUGHT

*If Saddler had been able to see himself now he would have been amazed at the transformation that had taken place over just a few short months. It has to be said that Mrs Saddler's cakes were something to write home about and living on a world where life for the most part meandered along in a pleasant, relaxed way didn't necessarily burn off too many calories. Not that Saddler had been unhealthy before, just maybe slightly rotund in a comfortable sort of way. The post Battle of Emajen Saddler had achieved things that hitherto would never have entered his wildest dreams. He was changed. Of that there was no doubt. Yet underneath it all the essential kind, caring, wonderful Saddler still remained. Nothing and no one could alter that…*

Once Saddler's heartrate had subsided, Champers aided him to sit up against the wall. Nub fussed over him, darting up and down his legs, arms and torso as though inspecting him to see what damage, if any, had been done. Her sharp little nose twitched rapidly as she searched his face to see if he were in pain. At length, apparently satisfied, she disappeared once more into his inside pocket, where he could feel her settling herself in. Champers meanwhile was washing his tail vigorously. Saddler was immediately concerned.

"Are you 'urt?" he queried.

Champers gave his tail one more lick and rested his golden eyes on Saddler.

"More ruffled," he replied with his usual calm. "Although you humans are remarkably heavy." He regarded Saddler seriously. "We need to press on. The longer we remain here, the more dangerous it will be. Whatever evil it is that resides down there will not rest until it has us in its clutches, body and spirit. Are you fit to carry on?"

Saddler nodded briskly. Now that his panic had dwindled, he felt stiff and rather bruised, but otherwise unscathed. The thought of those writhing fingers stealthily crawling their way back up the sides of the chasm was enough to get him on his feet.

"Let's go! I've 'ad enough of this place. I don't know 'ow you stand coming back 'ere voluntarily, like."

"One learns to adapt," Champers replied smoothly. "We both have a mission. Yours is to save Emajen. Mine, for the moment, is to help out however I can here."

Not usually given to tactile gestures, Champers patted a forepaw firmly on Saddler's back.

"You have withstood trials of both body and mind that many another would have quailed before. Keep courage, Saddler, you are so much stronger than you realize. Have belief in that strength. Why else would Crevitos have so desired to own you?"

This was a long speech for Champers and Saddler was deeply touched.

"Fank you," was all he could say.

Taking a deep breath, Saddler straightened his shoulders again and set off after Champers as he worked his way once more down the passageway.

Some while later, Saddler had lost count of the twists and turns as Champers made his way through the labyrinth of tunnels. How he had ever been able to find this route through the mines, was a total mystery to Saddler. For a while, they seemed to be on a continuing downward trend. The air grew staler by the minute and the cold became both damp and unremitting.

Finally, however, Saddler detected a slightly upward shift. Soon it became a steady uphill slope, and his legs began to ache with the effort of the unrelenting climb. At length his legs began to shake with sheer exertion as the incline became steeper. He stopped to catch his breath and called out to Champers, who was now some way ahead, to say he needed to stop just for a moment or two. As he called, Champers disappeared round a bend. Uncertain as to whether he'd been heard, Saddler was just about to push himself on when something dropped from the ceiling onto his shoulder. He felt it scuttle up his neck and into his hair.

"Ugh!" Frantically, Saddler rubbed at his hair to try to dislodge the creature. Even though he couldn't see what it was, he knew for certain it was one of the very same things, with far too many legs, that had scurried across his hand once before. While there were bound to be all sorts of small creatures in these mines, undoubtedly, they would be more scared of him than he of them, he reassured himself.

At that moment, a welcome orange glow played on the wall of the passage ahead. Saddler sighed with relief. Champers had realized he wasn't there and had come back to look for him, but his relief was short lived. He had barely put one foot in front of the other when another scuttling creature dropped on him from above - and another. Soon they were landing on him like droplets of rain. He could feel the multitude of scrabbling legs invading every inch of his body. They were everywhere - inside his jacket, up his sleeves, down his collar and under his cap. On and on, more fell from the ceiling. They weighed almost nothing at all individually, yet under their combined weight, Saddler felt his knees begin to buckle. He had been so shocked by the onslaught that he had barely moved. Now he thrust his hand inside his jacket in an effort to ward off any of the marauding creatures from reaching Nub.

He felt a sharp sting as he was bitten. It took all his strength of will not to snatch his hand away. All he could think under the assault was that he must protect Nub at all costs. Then there was light and noise. Saddler realized that Champers was yelling at him.

"Keep still, Saddler, keep still! They won't bite if you don't move."

For what seemed like hour upon hour, yet could barely have been moments, Saddler stood rock still. The hand that still shielded Nub throbbed painfully, and it was all he could do stop himself shuddering with revulsion at the feel of so many legs and prickly bodies assailing his every sense. Then it was over. Champers stood in front of him, holding some kind of bottle. As Saddler watched, a fine spray shot from the container and settled around him. As it did so, the last of the creatures hurried away from him and disappeared into the dark.

"You OK?" Champers said mildly.

"What was that?" Saddler was shaking from head to foot with disgust and loathing.

"Smicks. Revolting, scuttly things. Harmless enough on their own, but deadly in large gatherings - if they bite that is."

"Oh!" Saddler found it was all he could say.

"Fortunately, they hate the smell of chestnut oil. Always handy to have a bottle about one's person." Champers tucked the bottle into a small pouch hanging about his middle. "Shall we? Not too far, now."

Shell-shocked, Saddler meekly followed. He was almost beginning to wish he'd stayed in his nice, safe room, drawing Creations for Crevitos. But then, just the thought of that name lent extra strength to his legs. Determinedly, Saddler forged onwards.

# CHAPTER FIFTY- SIX
# HESITATION

*As Anthony listened to Saddler, he wondered how many other worlds there might be out there and whether they all had living creatures on them. He had always thought it was odd and probably unlikely that the planet Earth was the only world that supported life, even though current space exploration had yet to discover any anywhere else. But Emajen and Doodland weren't worlds that most people on Earth knew about. Were they in the solar system somewhere, he wondered? Or were they somehow on a different plane that could only be reached through – let's say it as it is – a magical gateway? It was really interesting, too, that creatures on Emajen and Earth had many similarities. Creations on Doodland, of course, had a strong link to Earth and so many shared Earth inhabitants' characteristics. It was all most intriguing…*

Finally, they had reached the top of the slope. According to Champers, the next right-hand passage would run for barely half a mile before it broadened into a small cave and thence out into Doomland. Saddler almost fancied that he could see a glimmer of light way down the passage. Impossible, of course, but it actually felt as though he might finally find a way out of this dire place.

"You should be fine from here on," said Champers.

"I'd never 'ave made it this far wivout you." Saddler stretched out his hand and grasped the forepaw raised to meet it. His fingers grasped fur that was silky soft; at the same time, he felt the roughness of warm, hard-working pads on his palm. It occurred to him then, what extraordinary creatures quaves were.

"I 'ope we shall meet again on Emajen in better circumstances."

"I'm sure so," Champers replied firmly. "Now, stick to the path and ignore the side passages. I must get back to Herbert. I don't like to leave him for too long. There's safety in numbers, as you have seen for yourself."

"Take care on the way back," said Saddler with concern.

The quave's whiskers twitched, almost as if he were smiling.

"I will do," he said gravely.

Farewells said, and with Nub on his shoulder, Saddler faced the final passageway that would lead him out of the mines. The darkness here was still just as impenetrable, but some of the menace had gone. Saddler travelled carefully, forcing himself to remain alert. Now, however, he trod with a lighter step. Once or twice, he passed a smaller passage branching to the left or right and a sinister waft of fetid air curled around him, assaulting his senses. This, however, he steadfastly ignored, anxious only to reach the end of this nightmare journey.

At last, there was a definite shift in the air. Every step became slightly warmer and fresher and Saddler's spirits lifted further. He knew his troubles would be far from over; he still had to find a safe place to use the gateway to Emajen. At least now though he felt certain that he would see Emajen again, even if what awaited him there meant more trouble still.

His thoughts now firmly on what lay ahead, Saddler had no warning and no time to react when something lunged at him from a side tunnel, knocking him flying. His lantern flew from his grasp, as Nub tumbled shrieking from his shoulder. Winded, all Saddler could do was scrabble crabwise into a small niche in the rock-face, where he sat trying to recover his breath. Straining to hear any sound of his assailant, he tensed briefly as something scurried up his arm, until he realized it was Nub.

"You alright?" he breathed softly. Nub rubbed his cheek with her head in reply.

"Can you see where it is?" Saddler whispered. He felt Nub slip back down his arm and he was surprised to find that he could discern her brief shadowy shape as she slipped around the corner of the rock. The light from the lantern had disguised the fact that there was, indeed, light at the end of the tunnel. Enough so that, now Saddler's eyes had had time to adjust, he was aware of the gloom and the shadows within the gloom, rather than the hitherto pitch black.

Nub was back. She tugged at his sleeve asking him to point with his own hand in the direction of whatever it was that had cannoned into him.

Cautiously, Saddler raised himself into a kneeling position. He could hear the thing shuffling around in the passage. Peering around the side of the rock, Saddler had to steady himself for a moment. He knew exactly what this was. Even in the murky gloom of the tunnel, there was no mistaking. The creature was around Saddler's own height and, even in the near dark, Saddler could see shadows where the creature's brittle scales merged and shifted as it shuffled about the passage.

Every so often, it collided with one wall or the other, then it would grunt and resume its shuffling again. This was clearly one of Crevitos's failed experiments. Saddler was pretty sure, too, that the poor creature was blind.

All at once, Saddler knew what he had to do. His heart quailed at the thought, but the creature stood between him and Emajen. There was no way Saddler could get out of this without a fight.

A battle to the death.

As silently as he could, Saddler crawled on hands and knees across the ground to where he could just make out the dim shape of the lantern. Matches at the ready, he had to hope against hope that the candle was still in one piece. Lighting the candle would undoubtedly alert the creature to his rough whereabouts, but he was pretty sure it wouldn't actually be able to see him. Watching the creature carefully as he edged forwards, Saddler finally reached the lamp. It had landed on one side, but fortunately seemed intact. Gingerly, Saddler set it to rights. He froze for a moment as it settled with a slight scraping noise against the rocky wall, but the creature continued to shuffle and search, seemingly oblivious. With shaking hands, Saddler took a match from its box. The scratching sound it made as the matchhead connected with the strip, seemed deafening in the gloom. He had barely a second to thrust the match through the door of the lantern before the creature had whipped round and came bowling at unexpected speed back down the corridor.

As it came, Saddler caught the glint of something metal hanging at its side. Saddler flung himself back towards the niche, leaving the lantern to illuminate the bizarre scene, but he was not quick enough. The creature might not be able to see, but it had other senses honed from years of living alone and abandoned in the darkness. Perhaps it detected Saddler's movement, or even perceived his fear. Whatever it was, it made a lunge in Saddler's direction. Rough hands connected with Saddler's jacket. With huge strength, Saddler was lifted clear off the ground and flung against the far wall. It felt as though every bone in his body must have shattered, yet fear drove him to his feet. The creature was lumbering towards him again. With horror, Saddler could see thick, rope-like tentacles unravelling from around its waist. Each one had an eye on its very tip. Each one of those eyes was looking directly at him!

Shock froze Saddler where he stood. He gazed at the apparition before him with horrified fascination. It was Nub squeaking that brought him to his senses. She had planted herself in front of the creature and was scolding in her shrill little voice. Each squirming eye was now focussed on her.

No time to stop and think. Nub had distracted the creature. Now Saddler had to act. He flung himself forwards through the slithering tendrils and grabbed for the sword that hung from the creature's side. With every ounce of strength that he could muster, Saddler wrenched the sword from its resting place. The creature, caught off balance, stumbled and crashed heavily to the floor. The tentacles writhed frantically, trying to latch onto Saddler, but he was able to leap backwards out of harm's way.

Finally he stood, sword poised, its tip at the unprotected throat of the creature - the Creation - laying helplessly before him.

Saddler paused for a long moment. He gazed at the Creation and his heart filled with pity. This was not the Creation's fault. This was Crevitos's doing - an experiment gone wrong. A creature left to wander in the dark, damaged and maimed by Crevitos's cruelty. What right had he, Saddler, to choose whether it should live or die?

Then the creature lifted its head with unseeing eyes which, nevertheless, looked right into Saddler's soul. Almost as though his hands were being guided by the Creation itself, Saddler plunged the sword downwards. In that instant, the creature's face softened and a look of immense peace spread across its features.

Saddler realized, guilt-ridden and sickened though he was, that he had finally set the Creation's tortured soul free!

# CHAPTER FIFTY - SEVEN
# BALM FOR THE SOUL

*It's a sobering thought that perhaps, given a unique set of circumstances, anyone might have it within them to take a life. There are creatures on Earth that many people dispatch without a second thought – spiders maybe, wasps, ants, flies – all kinds of things that are feared or threaten to overrun us if there are too many of them. Saddler was no different in that way than most humans, although he would prefer to find a way of removing pests if possible rather than killing them. But he would have staked his life on the fact that he couldn't kill another sentient being. Were Creations sentient? Of course they were. Look at Boff. He had thoughts and feelings the same as anyone else. Crevitos had an awful lot to answer for…*

Many parts of Saddler's Tale had been shocking, not to say distressing, but this last episode had left his friends dumbfounded beyond measure. This, for Saddler, was in essence the ultimate test of their friendship. He looked searchingly at each in turn, then his eyes rested on Boff and stayed there, beseeching understanding. As the only Creation in the group of friends, Saddler felt that Boff alone would really know, truly feel, the enormity of what Saddler had done.

Subsequently, in the battle of Emajen, many Creations had died and Saddler himself had been responsible for a number of those - well, all of them really, since it was he who had been able to point out the Creations' weakness in the first place. But that was war - a war that not one single inhabitant of Emajen had wanted.

Even now, though Saddler believed himself to be a peaceful man, he could barely recognize himself as the being who had led an army against Crevitos and, in doing so, had helped to save his world. But his actions in that dim, dark passageway had been something else again. Saddler was still not sure whether it was through his own choice that he had plunged the Creation's own sword deep into its unprotected throat. Nonetheless, he had done it! And only he could take responsibility for his actions.

Boff, thankfully, was unequivocal in his reaction. He could see the anguish behind Saddler's eyes and wished for nothing more than to make it go away. He flashed Saddler his triangular grin and his lightbulbs flickered.

"Thank you, Saddler," was what he said.

"Sterling work, if you ask me," interjected a slightly gravelly voice.

"I couldn't have put it better myself," agreed another in a softer, silkier tone.

Everyone turned almost as one to gaze at the two newcomers framed in the archway.

Nebiré smiled widely. "Welcome, friends," she intoned.

"Herbert and Champers, if I'm not much mistaken," said the Prof.

Saddler glanced at Nebiré. "You...?"

"Of course," she replied softly.

Saddler sat back and watched as his friends, his wonderful, unbelievable, incredible friends drew the newcomers into their midst and made them welcome. Champers and Herbert were just what the group had needed to break the intense spell of darkness that had dogged Saddler's tale through the mines. For the moment, he felt drained by its retelling, and he was content just to sit and bask in the soothing radiance of such staunch friendship.

Boff's smile had told Saddler what he wanted to know, perhaps now his own tormented soul could begin to heal.

He closed his eyes and listened to the gentle hubbub around him, his mind wandering back to the moment that he had finally emerged from Doomland's tortuous mines. The final part of his tale was still to be told, but for now Saddler was content to remain just as he was.

# CHAPTER FIFTY-EIGHT
# TIME IS OF THE ESSENCE

*It was important to Boff that he communicate to Saddler exactly how he was feeling. Boff had seen Saddler looking at him with an anguished expression as he recounted killing the Creation in the mines. But Boff had to make Saddler see that he understood. There had been no choice then, and there had been no choice during the Battle of Emajen either. Those Creations had been stripped of their will and their essence by Crevitos and were doomed to an existence of misery and violence, only to be discarded if they no longer served Crevitos's purpose. Boff knew that Saddler would carry that guilt with him always, but hoped his empathy would help to ease that burden in some small way…*

Daylight was never exactly light on Doomland - it was as if the whole of that world had plunged into the slough of despond once Crevitos had brutally made it his own. Most likely, it was the constant belching of fumes and dust from the vast fires that raged within the mines, that clouded the atmosphere and ravaged the landscape - the effect was the same. Nevertheless, nearing the entrance to the cave, Saddler found himself squinting; after the darkness of the mines, the light was still enough to hurt his eyes. All at once, he found he was shaking uncontrollably - reaction to the encounter with the Creation, perhaps, or even relief at being out of the mines. Slowly, Saddler lowered himself to the ground. He rested his back against the cave wall and closed his eyes for a moment or two. Nub sat on his shoulder and rubbed his ear softly in her small, comforting way. Compared to the atmosphere in the mines, the air here was positively fresh. Saddler breathed it in slowly and deeply, reassured by the coolness of it on his skin and by the wan light that played across his closed eyelids. They stayed this way together, Nub and he, just for a short while, until Saddler felt his joints begin to stiffen and various aches creeping into his bruised and battered muscles and bones.

Saddler pursed his lips. "Better be makin' a move," he remarked softly. Nub stroked his cheek with her paw and snuggled into his neck, sighing. Saddler opened his eyes and groaned as he stiffly clambered to his feet. Cautiously, he peered around the entrance to the cave. Far away to his left, he could see the towering fortress that he had, for a short while (unbelievably) called home.

The long, slatted, wooden bridge that led up to the entrance was a hive of activity. Creations scurried here, there and everywhere. There were distant shouts, the clang of metal, the rumble of wheels; indeed, it struck Saddler immediately, all the bustle and noise you might expect from an army preparing for war.

Then his heart froze.

A figure appeared. A tall imposing figure. A figure Saddler knew only too well.

With his heart now pounding painfully in his chest, Saddler watched Crevitos stop and cast his eyes over the landscape, as though searching for something. His gaze turned in Saddler's direction and lingered there just a moment too long - or so it seemed to Saddler. He shrank back, trembling, into the cave. There was absolutely no way Crevitos could know that he was there, he reassured himself. Nonetheless, he could clearly picture the cruel smile flitting across Crevitos's features, and an involuntary shudder shook his body from head to toe.

Summoning every ounce of courage he could muster, Saddler edged very, very slowly around the side of the cave entrance once more - just enough to be able to see, without being seen. Nothing had changed. There was no posse of Creations storming in his direction, and Saddler realized now that there was no way Crevitos would have been able to see him, even in the unlikely event that it had crossed his mind to wonder if Saddler were there.

Crevitos himself was no longer in evidence - a fact that might, or might not, be seen as a blessing. One thing was certain though, Saddler needed to get moving. The longer he stayed here, the more likely the chance of being discovered. Crevitos was back, and there were unmistakable signs that he was mobilizing his army. Saddler needed to get back to Emajen - fast!

To the right of the cave, the mountainous terrain stretched as far as the eye could see. It was desolate; there was no sign of life at all. There would be plenty of cover; hopefully Saddler would be able to find somewhere safe to use the gateway, without having to travel too far.

Such light as there was, was beginning to wane. If he didn't make a move now, Saddler would almost certainly have to spend the night in the cave - a prospect he most definitely didn't relish. Hitching his backpack up on his shoulders, Saddler rested Nub in the palm of his hand and gave her a sad smile.

"I don't 'ave no words, Nub." He stroked the little creature softly with his finger. "We've been through some stuff, you and me, but I 'ave to go - I 'ave to 'elp save Emajen. Or at least try."

Nub's eyes grew persuasively large and round, boring a hole into Saddler's heart.

"I can't take you wiv me. It would be wrong. There's gonna be fighting, and I don't even know if I'll still be around at the end of it!"

Nub remained uncharacteristically silent. Her eyes grew rounder still.

"Besides," Saddler continued desperately, "This is your 'ome. The mines are your 'ome…"

Nub tilted her tiny head coquettishly to one side, as though she'd listened to his arguments and remained unconvinced.

Saddler threw his arms up in defeat. "Well, as long as it's your decision," he said helplessly.

Nub scurried up his arm, headbutted his chin affectionately and disappeared into her usual place inside his jacket. Concerned on the one hand, but secretly overjoyed, Saddler scoured the landscape to the right of the cave once more. With a hopeful heart, he set off to find a place where he could, undetected, use the gateway that Nebiré had given him.

He was going home. At last, he was going back to Emajen.

# CHAPTER FIFTY-NINE
# LIGHT AND DARK

*Nobody knew how the gateway between worlds worked. Even Nebiré had no knowledge of its origins, or when, or how the first gateway had come into existence. The fact that each gateway was contained within a small, ornate, wooden box was also puzzling. It had taken all of Nebiré's considerable powers to work out how to transfer a small portion of the gateway's formidable energy into the pouch she gave to Saddler. She knew it was risky and very possibly wouldn't work, but it was the only way she could think of to help Saddler get back to Emajen…*

It didn't take Saddler very long to scramble his way across the rough ground before finding himself completely out of sight of the fortress. Rocky protuberances and spears, some soaring hundreds of feet up into the sky, dotted the landscape as far as the eye could see. Saddler clambered a short way up the craggy hillside, until he was fairly sure he would be totally hidden from view behind one of these strange, soaring projections. Stopping to catch his breath, he surveyed the land around him. There was nothing to see - no signs of life anywhere. This, he figured, was a good a place as any.

There was still the possibility that someone would see the flash of light as he opened the pouch containing the gateway Nebiré had given him. When he had passed through a gateway before, Saddler had always been careful not to be seen because of the sudden brightness of the light followed swiftly by the ebony inkblot of darkness that it produced. He had no way of knowing how bright or expansive the light created by his small pouch might be. However, it was a risk he would have to take. Delaying much longer seemed to pose a greater risk than the faint possibility that someone would see the very brief burst of brightness the gateway emitted.

Saddler patted his pocket.

"This is it, Nub," he said softly.

A thrill of excitement knotted his stomach and sent ripples of nervous anticipation coursing through his veins.

"It might feel a bit strange, but it won't last long!" he told Nub reassuringly.

There was no response from his pocket, so he patted it gently once more before carefully retrieving the pouch from his backpack.

For a second or two, Saddler held the pouch cautiously in front of him. This was such a strange feeling, such a complex droplet in the pool of time. On the one hand, this was just a tiny thing, a simple action he had performed on numerous occasions:

on the other, it was a momentous occasion and one which he had thought for so very, very long, would never happen.

For a split second, a tendril of doubt wormed its way across his thoughts. Supposing the gateway didn't work? Supposing he had taken too long getting to this point, and it had run out of power? Nebiré had said it was only temporary and that she wasn't sure how effective it might be on this world. Supposing it worked, but took him somewhere else altogether - or, worse still, flipped him right back into the fortress? All kinds of dark possibilities began to assail Saddler's thoughts. A veil of shadow clouded his eyes and he cried out in horror as the chaos of warring doubts in his mind reached fever pitch. Saddler thrust his hands in the air, clutching at his head to still the pandemonium raging inside his skull.

As he did so, the pouch slipped from his grasp.

Slowly, it fell… a feather, drifting silently downwards… a leaf hovering on a gentle breeze… Still and calm, it descended while Saddler battled the tumultuous forces within him.

Until, connecting with the rugged ground, the pouch burst open and a tremendous, searing brightness obliterated the landscape. At that same moment, a familiar cruel smile invaded Saddler's mind, just as the gateway turned from light to dark.

Saddler felt himself being pulled by something, some inexplicable force, and he stumbled forwards. A word filled his head, obliterating all else and he cried out again in pain and despair.

"EMAJEN!"

The darkness closed around him, and he felt himself being tossed and tumbled within it, in a way that he had never experienced before. But as his body plunged and plummeted, his mind began to clear. The darkness lifted.

Four powerful arms embraced him and steadied him, as his feet touched the ground. Then he was held at arm's length and he gazed at the beautiful, wonderful, beloved heart-shaped face of Nebiré.

"A bit of a rocky ride!" Saddler said shakily, "But I got 'ere. Not too late I 'ope!"

Nebiré's face lit up in a radiant smile.

"Not too late, Saddler," she replied. "Welcome back to Emajen. Welcome home!"

# CHAPTER SIXTY
# HEALING

*Although there are many similarities between animals on Earth and animals on Emajen, many of the creatures on Emajen have the ability to talk, which those on Earth do not. This has its advantages and disadvantages (as is also the case with human beings!) but it does mean that most animals on Emajen are fairly laid back, because you can explain things to them. The Natorqua however, though able to talk, did so extremely rarely, preferring more of a mind transference of their thoughts – similar to what we know on Earth as telepathy. When Saddler returned to Emajen, he had no idea what effect Crevitos's meddling might have had on the remaining Natorqua's minds. In fact he was very afraid indeed of what he might find…*

There was much to be done and much to be discussed, but Saddler was clearly exhausted both mentally and physically by the traumas he had been through. Nub, too, looked rather dishevelled from the tumultuous journey through the gateway in Saddler's pocket.

As with all creatures, Nub was instantly smitten with Nebiré, and Saddler had to confess to a slight pang of jealousy as she willingly allowed Nebiré to fuss over her, finding her food and smoothing her ruffled fur. However, when Nebiré settled Saddler into a vast, soft, cosy bed, Nub immediately snuggled up next to him on the pillow and instantly fell asleep.

"Here," Nebiré offered Saddler a small draft she'd prepared. "This will at least take some of the sting out of your aches and pains while you sleep."

Saddler smiled grimly. "As if I 'aven't 'ad enough potions to drink for one lifetime!" he said ruefully. Nonetheless, he took the proffered drink gratefully, his trust in Nebiré absolute.

***

How long he slept for, Saddler had no way of knowing, but he awoke feeling wonderfully refreshed. Stretching his limbs carefully, he was amazed to feel barely any stiffness at all. True to her word, Nebiré's potion had done its job while he slept, and he felt ready to face the challenges yet to come. He was also, he discovered with some surprise, ravenously hungry. As if she had read his thoughts, Nebiré appeared carrying a tray full of tea things and a wonderful selection of mouth-watering snacks.

Nub now rode on her shoulder and squeaked with delight when she saw that Saddler was awake. With her usual exuberance, Nub leapt from Nebiré's shoulder and proceeded to cover his face with nibbles and licks until, laughing, he had to beg her to stop.

Nebiré set the tea things next to the bed, as Saddler swung his legs out to sit on the edge. Wheezing slightly, she sat down next to him. While he ate, she spoke to him of what she had been able to glean of his travels through the mines, although much of it had been very unclear. Between mouthfuls, Saddler had filled in the gaps. Nebiré probed gently, asking of Saddler only that he felt comfortable to tell.

When he finally reached the point in his tale where he had seen Crevitos on the bridge, Nebiré's smooth brow had wrinkled with concern. Just the thought of Crevitos made Saddler feel slightly nauseous and he pushed the last few mouthfuls of food away uneaten. Nebiré used all four arms to lever herself up from the bed, and she stood, hands on hips, looking solemnly at Saddler.

"I trust you are rested now, Saddler - it seems events are about to overtake us quicker than I'd hoped."

She then began to tell Saddler what she had seen through the crystal web.

"As you suspected, Crevitos has found a way to bring his army through a gateway into Emajen. From what you say, he is wasting no time organizing his troops ready to descend on our beloved world. There will be a battle, that much is certain - how it will end, that I cannot see, or perhaps the crystals will not show me."

"What am I doing 'ere then, lazing about and stuffing me face?" Saddler said aghast.

Nebiré allowed herself a small smile. "You need to be strong for what lies ahead, Saddler. The short time you have taken to recuperate will have no bearing on what comes next."

Saddler stood up briskly and groaned involuntarily as various parts of his anatomy now twinged in complaint.

"I only wish we had more time to heal you completely!" Nebiré remarked sympathetically.

"You've 'elped me more than you know," Saddler said firmly.

Actually, Nebiré almost certainly did know, as she seemed to know practically everything, but Saddler was determined not to show any signs of weakness now. He was fed and watered. He was rested. His body was in as good a shape as possible given the circumstances. And he was back on Emajen; that in itself was the greatest healer of all. He had a job to do, even though he wasn't yet entirely sure what that might entail. All that had happened before must be carefully stored away in the furthest vaults of his mind, until the right time came to remember it again. For now, he had to focus on the present and concentrate every ounce of his strength on trying to save Emajen.

Saddler looked at Nebiré.

"I'm ready!" he said.

"Good!" she replied. "Come, then. I have something to show you."

# CHAPTER SIXTY-ONE
# ASTONISHING DEVELOPMENTS

*On Emajen all living beings are sentient – that is to say they have consciousness, perception and feeling in the same way that humans do. Many people on Earth believe that trees are sentient. Trees on Emajen most definitely are. Saddler knew from Nebiré that each and every tree had a spirit and that some were so old they had been there since before her time – which was a very long time indeed…*

Saddler had never before witnessed the way the trees responded to Nebiré as she made her way amongst them. It was a tremendous sight to behold. Saddler knew that every tree had its spirit, but he hadn't actually seen them come alive as they did when Nebiré was in their midst. They were almost animated, although if you stopped to look directly at any particular tree, it looked just like a tree. Collectively though, it was more a sense of their aliveness, somewhere on the edge of his vision. There were shiftings and sighings, rustlings and swayings, and a feeling of such intense energy it almost took his breath away.

Periodically, Nebiré would stop to catch her breath and the most amazing thing of all would happen. Trees on either side of the path would dip their branches, lifting her gently as though she were a fragile flower. For a little way, they would pass her one to the other along the path until, at some unseen signal, they would set her gently down once more and, murmuring her thanks, Nebiré would continue slowly along the path.

The trees seemed to have a new deference for Saddler too, or at least that was how he felt. Many a time he had traversed this wood to see his great friend, and on every occasion the trees would poke a little harmless fun: changing the path; sticking a root up to make him stumble; or pinging his cap off with a carefully placed branch. Saddler had never minded, knowing it was all done in friendly jest. He knew that the woods were more than capable of protecting Nebiré if the need arose. He had never seen them angry - perhaps there was rarely any need for them to be - but he was pretty sure he wouldn't want to be around if they were.

Now, however, he was convinced that the roots were shrinking back into the path as he walked. The path itself seemed broader, and not a single branch, or twig, hindered his advance. Once, as they stopped, a leafy twig gently stroked his cheek and when he turned to look at the tree, he was convinced it was smiling.

After so many trials, so much testing of mind and body, Saddler found this walk through the woods soothing and healing, as though every step he took mended one of the plethora of rents and tears in his worn and weary soul.

Finally, they reached the far edge of the woods. Before they stepped out into the open countryside, Nebiré placed her hand lightly on Saddler's arm.

"Are you sure you're ready for this, Saddler?"

Saddler took a deep breath, filling his lungs with the freshness of the day. He drew in positive energy from the trees, closing his eyes for a moment to relish the feelings of strength and calm that flowed through him.

"Nope!"

"That's good," chuckled Nebiré. "Then you will be focussed and alert. We will all face this together, whatever it may be."

Together they stepped out into the sunlight. What Saddler beheld caused him to gasp with wonder and amazement. Stretched before him, as far as the eye could see, inhabitants of Emajen bustled about in a hive of activity amongst makeshift dwellings. All were busy; all intent on preparations for the biggest threat Emajen had ever faced.

Glancing up, first one and then another noticed Saddler and Nebiré standing there. Fingers, paws, tentacles, all manner of creatures pointing and shouting across to their friends and neighbours, until every being there had stopped what they were doing and were looking in Saddler's direction. The noise hushed. Even the birds stilled their song. There was silence as Saddler gazed at the vast hordes of beings blanketing the countryside, and they gazed expectantly back at him.

Then, without warning, a huge cheer arose and was carried in great waves across the sea of Emajen's people. Saddler's heart swelled with joy and pride. He had never expected this. He knew Nebiré had talked about raising any army, but never in his wildest imaginings had he envisaged such a vast throng of people, creatures, Creations - every being imaginable.

Saddler turned to Nebiré, only to find that she was no longer there. He smiled to himself. Nebiré had her own part still to play; he however had to face his hardest challenge yet.

Turning, Saddler walked steadily down the hillside to the waiting throng below and disappeared into the welcoming crowd.

# CHAPTER SIXTY-TWO
# A SOMBRE MOMENT

*So much had happened in such a short time, that it was really quite hard to take it all in. Despite Destiny's early misgivings, Emajen had almost become like a second home. Saddler, Nebiré, all of them were like family she'd known forever, not just a few short months. Their journey to find the Natorqua, their involvement in the Battle of Emajen, and now the incredible tale that Saddler had told them were over. Things, relatively speaking, were going back to normal. Which was good, of course. Better than good. But also sad in a way, because what happened now? Did she and Anthony have any part to play in Emajen's future? She almost couldn't bear it if this turned out to be a final goodbye…*

And there you 'ave it," Saddler said with a sigh of relief. It was over. He had told his tale, warts and all. He had missed nothing out, spared them no detail, because they were his friends and they had a right to know.

"We'd 'ad very little time to prepare ourselves, and nuffink much in the way of weapons, so to speak - not been much call for that sort of fing 'ere before. But what I did 'ave, was knowledge: knowledge about 'ow to um… well… defeat Crevitos's abominations."

"You knew their weak spots," chipped in Anthony.

"Yeah, and lucky I did, otherwise we'd 'ave 'ad no chance. As it was, we still would 'ave lost if you two 'adn't been able to connect wiv the Natorqua and give the herd back its strength."

There was quiet for a moment as everyone reflected on that momentous day (could it have been bare months ago?) when Crevitos had invaded Emajen. Looking back, it seemed as though it must have been some freakish nightmare - one they had all shared. Yet, it seemed that even a peaceful world such as Emajen could be threatened by evil.

On the face of it, after the battle, all had returned to the way it was before. The Natorqua had resumed being the serene, beautiful, mystical creatures they had always been before Crevitos had tried to destroy them. And because of this, Emajen's balance had also been restored. As before, inhabitants of Emajen could wander freely amongst the Natorqua and feel strengthened and calmed by their presence.

Now, more than ever, Emajen's inhabitants cherished their Natorqua. Perhaps, before the battle, they had rather taken for granted that the Natorqua were there. If that were so, then it was the case no longer. The Natorqua were Emajen's lifeblood, and those who maybe hadn't appreciated it before, certainly did so now. So, yes, Emajen had been restored, but the battle had left its scars too. There was no way it could not. Saddler himself was no longer quite the same old Saddler, although the intervening months (and it had to be said, Mrs Saddler's rather excellent cooking) had restored some of the rosiness to his cheeks and a notch or two on his belt. And, of course, not all of Emajen's inhabitants had survived the great battle, as is the inevitability of war.

The group were silent and the mood was solemn for a short while, as thoughts of the Battle of Emajen, and all it had meant for this world, played across their minds.

At length, Destiny sighed. "Thank you for telling us your story, Saddler. It must have been so hard to do."

Nebiré shifted in her wicker chair. "And as Saddler's tale ends, so your time here does too."

"Oh, I was so hoping we might be able to see the Natorqua again!" Destiny's eyes filled involuntarily with tears. "Will you come for us again, Saddler?"

Saddler shook his head seriously. "Nah! Who'd want you pair galumphing round Emajen, disturbing the peace!"

Destiny's eyes opened wide, and her mouth formed an 'O' of surprise. Then she felt Anthony's gentle shove on her shoulder and his fond exclamation of, "Chump!" just as Saddler's face broke into a wide, playful, very Saddleresque grin.

"Saddler!" Destiny laughed at herself, and the solemn mood was broken.

"Time to go, but before we do, I fink Boff 'as somefink 'e wants to give you two."

Anthony and Destiny looked enquiringly at Boff, who rooted about under his cushion and produced a wooden box. It wasn't terribly large, but it was covered in intricate, carved patterns, which spoke of mysterious secrets inside. In the small lock was an ornate key, which shimmered slightly to the discerning eye.

Anthony and Destiny exchanged a glance.

"Is that what…" Anthony began.

"We think it is?" concluded Destiny.

Boff held the innocuous little box out towards them. Nobody would ever guess that such a simple looking object harboured a gateway between worlds!

"I don't need it." Boff smiled his triangular smile. "Emajen is my home now, and I know if I want to visit Doodland, I only have to ask Nebiré or the Prof, or Saddler to borrow one of their gateways. This way, you can visit us whenever you like."

Anthony and Destiny both looked at Nebiré, whose one purple eye twinkled.

"With my blessing," she rumbled.

Destiny hugged Boff. "You're a star!" she told him.

Boff grinned his triangular grin and his light bulbs flashed happily.

"Thanks, Boff!" Anthony hugged him. "We'll take very good care of it, too." They then said their adieus (not, of course, actual goodbyes) before setting off once more to Saddler's house: Mrs Saddler would be mortally wounded if they didn't stop by for a quick cup of tea and a slice of cake before heading home.

# CHAPTER SIXTY-THREE
# REFLECTIONS

*There were no two ways about it, Anthony reflected once Saddler's tale was complete, their time on Emajen had been epic to say the least. In Anthony's opinion, no one in their right mind would ever want to be involved in a war, let alone start one, but he had to admit that the whole quest, the friendships they'd forged and the trials he and Destiny had faced had changed his perspective on life completely. Adversity had made them grow in ways they might not have done otherwise. It had given them confidence and made them stronger to face whatever the future might have in store for them…*

As they walked at a leisurely pace through Nebiré's wood, Destiny wandered a little ahead, humming to herself. Every so often, she would lay a hand on a tree trunk, or gently caress a newly forming leaf. Since being on Emajen, she had become much more aware of all life around her; much more conscious of how incredible and astounding things were; things that she had really always just taken for granted. True, she was an ardent lover of animals and passionate about their welfare, but she had never really stopped to ask herself why. Now she found herself mesmerized by the smallest of details: the way her rabbits stretched and yawned; the way the patterns formed symmetrically on her tortoises' shells, or the incredibly intricate web of blood-vessels she could see in her cats' ears when the sunlight shone through them.

Destiny had always loved trees too and walking through woods, but Nebiré's trees had taught her to look so much closer. Of course, the trees on Earth didn't respond quite the same as those on Emajen did; it saddened Destiny to think that over the years they had withdrawn into themselves and away from human beings, who often misused them so casually. Walking through Nebiré's woods in the sunshine, was a little cameo of joy: they were surrounded by birdsong and knew that Emajen was safe and well once again.

Behind Destiny, Anthony and Saddler walked together.

"That's quite some story you had to tell," Anthony said. "Are you OK, Saddler? I mean, really OK, after everything you've been through?"

Saddler thought for a moment and a slight frown wrinkled his brow. "I 'ave to be one of the luckiest beings alive," he began thoughtfully. "I live in this fabulous world, and I definitely 'ave the best friends anyone ever 'ad. I know Emajen is safe now, too, so whatever 'appened to me in the past, don't really matter."

"But…" prompted Anthony.

"But, I guess - for me at least - fings can never be quite the same. There's always just that niggling in the back of me mind - what if somefink like that 'appened again."

Anthony nodded sympathetically. There was really nothing he could say. From all his dealings with rescue horses, he knew that it took a long, long time and an infinite amount of patience to undo the physical and mental torture some of them had been through. With the right care and love, most of them would come right and learn to trust again. But that trust was always fragile and easy to break. You could never entirely erase the past.

"Any'ow, that's quite enough of me! I did just 'appen to notice, as we was all saying our goodbyes, that Nebiré was a mite distracted. I 'ave a feeling she was up to somefink."

They were nearing the edge of the woods now, and Anthony thought he caught a glimpse of something bright that shimmered as it caught the sunlight.

With a big smile on his face, he glanced up at Saddler. "I think you're right, and I'm pretty sure I know what, too."

Hastening their steps, the two of them caught up with Destiny. Linking arms with his dearest friend, Anthony gave her an affectionate squeeze. Together, the three of them stepped through the trees.

# CHAPTER SIXTY-FOUR
# JOY

*As the others departed, Nebiré hummed to herself. For now, things on Emajen were as they should be. All was right with her world, apart from one small shadow: Crevitos. Where was he now? The crystals gave her no hint that he had any part to play in Emajen's future. For that she was grateful. But that didn't mean he might not be somewhere plotting some other world's demise. They could only hope against hope that he would never have the strength to rise again…*

Destiny gasped. She shut her eyes and reopened them again, just in case she was dreaming. No dream, but a glorious, wonderful, heart-stopping sight. Across the fields, at the bottom of the hill, the herd of Natorqua grazed peacefully in the sunlight. It was a truly magical scene. As they gazed across at the herd, Destiny was struck yet again by their majestic beauty: how it was that both horse and cat features merged and blended to form a creature of such power and such graceful beauty. She found it hard to comprehend.

On Earth, cats were predators and horses were prey - how could it be then that they could create one sublime being of such magnificence? It was a paradox.

"The herd seems to have grown," she said softly, not wanting to break the spell of peace that the Natorqua inevitably weaved around them.

Antony pointed. "Look!" he said. "Haven't you noticed?"

Destiny followed the direction of his hand and her eyes widened with joy.

"Foals," she cried, totally forgetting to be quiet. Only one regal head raised itself calmly to look in their direction. There was a single, gentle wicker, and the Alpha-Female resumed her grazing.

"I fink we've just been invited to go and join her," said Saddler.

Making their way down the sloping hillside, they were soon in amongst the herd. They could feel the incredible energy that radiated from the Natorqua all around them. As they reached the Alpha-Female, she lifted her head once more and blew softly at them through her nostrils. From the shelter of her flank, a small head appeared and Destiny gave a squeak of delight.

"Oh! May I? May I, please?" she breathed. The Alpha-Female nudged her youngster forwards. Shyly, it responded to Destiny's soothing voice and sniffed at her outstretched hand. Within moments, it was following her every move, nudging her to play if she so much as stopped to take a breath.

Anthony watched, laughing. With experienced hands, he caressed the Alpha-Female, very quickly discovering that the Natorqua, like horses, have a favourite 'itchy spot'.

"Clever, as well as beautiful," he said, looking at the foal. He was rewarded by a playful nudge as the Alpha-Female leaned in to enjoy the scratching just a little more.

Saddler watched the children with a lump in his throat. For this, he would re-live every single moment of the pain and fear Crevitos had inflicted on him. For this, it had all been worthwhile.

Finally, the Natorqua called her foal to her and the herd began to drift away. Destiny, Anthony and Saddler walked quietly alongside them until their paths diverged. With one final cuddle for the foal, they thanked the Alpha-Female and watched her meander off into the distance.

"Nebiré's doing," remarked Saddler.

"I guessed as much," beamed Destiny. "Thank her for us, when you see her next, please, Saddler!"

"I will, of course. I'm betting that she already knows though.

# CHAPTER SIXTY-FIVE
# RANDOMNESS

*Destiny and Anthony had often discussed why it was that different worlds didn't seem to interconnect. Saddler had long ago explained to them that Earth and Emajen had forged different paths and that Earth humans had a reputation for being destructive. Anthony thought it could be good for worlds to help each other and share positive things like medicines and knowledge, but Destiny wasn't so sure. If anything, Earth's history showed that humans were always looking to invade parts of the world that didn't belong to them and take far more than they needed from the Earth's resources. Saddler had been adamant he didn't want that to happen on Emajen. After all that had happened with Crevitos (who, let's face it, was created by a human) Anthony was beginning to see Saddler's point…*

With promises to visit often, Anthony and Destiny hugged Saddler and Mrs Saddler and breathed in one last breath of sweet, fresh Emajen air, before opening their special box and slipping through the gateway back to Earth.

It was almost light when they reappeared once more in the greenhouse and the birds were in full flow of their rousing dawn chorus. By some unspoken, mutual consent, both children said nothing. They had so much to discuss, but for now they were both tired and ready to crash for a short couple of hours. It would be difficult to sleep with all that Saddler had told them rattling around in their minds, but there was time enough to mull it all over later.

***

Back here on Earth, today was going to be a big day. Anthony's dad, Matt, having been to see the rescue horse, had agreed to take it back to the ranch in America. Originally, Anthony had heard via a friend at school, all about the poor animal. Nonetheless, when his dad had come back from his first visit to see it, neither Anthony nor Destiny had been prepared for the description Matt gave them, or the photos of the state the poor creature was in.

Physically, for the month the horse had been with its current saviour, Mr Stovriec, it had improved hugely. Mentally, however, it was traumatized, and Mr Stovriec felt he did not have the expertise to help it to recover sufficiently.

A seemingly complex web of discussions between Anthony's friend Mia, Mia's father, Mr Stovriec, Anthony himself and Anthony's dad had led to this point where the horse was now going to go to the ranch in America, where it had the best possible chance of rehabilitation.

It seemed like the perfect solution.

Destiny's mum had been intrigued by the whole situation. "Funny how these things work out," she had said, when Destiny first told her about it. "Has Mia's father known Mr Stovriec long?"

"No. I think he only moved to the area a couple of months ago. He must be a really nice man though - apparently, he didn't know too much about horses before, but felt desperately sorry when he came across this one. He brought it home and started looking after it!"

"There are some good people in the world!" Jenny said wryly, knowing full well Destiny's view on people who maltreated animals.

"I know mum, it's just that there are too many cruel ones."

***

So, today was the day that Matt was due to pick up the horse. He had agreed that Anthony and Destiny could go with him. It was to be an early start, which was why Anthony and Destiny were keen to grab an hour or two's sleep.

However, just as Anthony was about to step around the trees that separated the greenhouse area from the rest of the garden, he caught a glimpse of movement across the kitchen window. Hurriedly, he held out a restraining hand to stop Destiny in her tracks.

"What…?"

"Well that's awkward," said Anthony.

"What is?"

Cautiously, Anthony peered once more around the tree. Dad was now standing at the back door, with a mug of coffee in hand, breathing in the early morning air.

"Dad's already up!" he whispered.

"It's four-thirty in the morning!" she squeaked incredulously.

"Yeah! You know what dad's like. He'll be going over every last detail in his mind. It's not at all easy shipping a horse across to America. He'll want to be certain that nothing is left to chance."

"So, what are we going to do now? I don't fancy standing here for the next two hours until he decides to have a shower or something."

Anthony cast around him for inspiration, then grinned. Ducking down, he appeared to be scrabbling around in the undergrowth. Finally, he resurfaced with a handful of dandelion leaves.

"We blag it, as always!" he said. "We were both woken early by the dawn chorus, and you decided, quite randomly, which is exactly like you, that we should go foraging for tortoise food. It's perfect!"

Destiny opened her mouth to object, then laughed. Anthony was right. It was exactly the kind of random thing she would do. There were no holds barred where her animals were concerned. As it turned out, Matt's mind was understandably elsewhere. He didn't bat an eyelid at their rambling explanation for why they were in the garden at four-thirty in the morning, if indeed he really took it on board at all. He did suggest, much to their relief, that the pair of them grab a couple more hours of sleep as it was going to be a stressful day.

# CHAPTER SIXTY-SIX
# THE END?

*Crevitos paced. It was something he did without realising he did it. A habit born of a seemingly endless reservoir of energy which simply needed an outlet.*

*Had it been so much to ask, he mused? A little world domination. A chance to be powerful beyond imagining. So much time, so much planning and preparation gone to waste. He sucked in a deep breath, held it and then let it hiss back out between his teeth. He paused for a moment by the window, gazing through it at the fields beyond without actually seeing them. His chin came up determinedly. No use crying over spilt milk. There were lessons to be learned from defeat and he was a quick learner. A cruel, calculating smile played across his lips: it was to his advantage that those who had engineered his downfall didn't know if he yet lived, but if they thought Crevitos was beaten, they were very much mistaken.*

*There was always another world to conquer…*

Finally, they were in the horse box and on their way to collect the rescue horse. The plan was that Anthony and Destiny would travel with Matt to the airport where Destiny's mum would meet up with them. She would then bring them back once Matt was on his way.

Destiny was nervous. The reason for their ridiculously early start was that they had no idea how the horse might react to being loaded into the horse box. It had been in such a poor state when Mr Stovriec had had it transported to him, that it hadn't had the strength of mind or body to object. Now, though, there would have to be some careful handling if the horse wouldn't load. It could take as much as a couple of hours of careful trust building to calmly persuade the animal onto the ramp and into the box.

This was where Anthony came in useful. He had such an amazing way with horses, even the most distrustful of them would soon respond to his firm kindness. He knew a huge range of techniques, having worked with Merlin at the ranch nearly every school holiday for the past six years. It was incredible how he could encourage the most nervous of horses to trust him.

Thankfully, it was no more than a half hour drive to Mr Stovriec's smallholding. The horse box was soon trundling up a short, stone driveway. At his dad's instruction, Anthony leaped out to open a sturdy five-bar gate and the horse box slowly made its way around the back of a pretty rose-covered cottage to an immaculate stable-yard.

"Wow!" said Destiny, impressed. "I thought Mr Stovriec didn't know anything about keeping horses."

"Apparently, the stable yard was already here. I believe he was planning to demolish it before our equine friend melted his heart."

Destiny smiled appreciatively. She had a feeling she was going to like Mr Stovriec. In her mind's eye, he looked a little bit like Saddler, with the same kindly expression in his eyes.

Having suitably parked the horse box, Matt, Anthony and Destiny made their way back around to the front of the cottage and rang the bell.

After a moment or two, they heard approaching footsteps and the door swung slowly inwards. As the occupant of the house stepped forward into the light, Destiny's mouth dropped open, her face turning a sickly shade of whitish-grey. Clumsily, she stumbled backwards into Anthony. His expression, too, was a picture of disbelief, as he grabbed Destiny to stop her from falling.

"Welcome!" Mr Stovriec's voice was smooth as he held out his hand to Matt, but his gaze, and that mocking smile were fixed firmly on the children. It was a cruel, yet beautiful visage Destiny remembered only too well seeing once before in the clouds.

Saddler, too, had described that sardonic expression, so clearly and in such detail that neither Anthony nor Destiny were in any doubt as to who this really was.

And the chances of this being a coincidence were?

Precisely nil!

And the likelihood that there was unimaginable trouble brewing was?

A sure-fire certainty!

Mr Stovriec placed a supposedly friendly hand on Matt's shoulder and, gesturing towards the back of the house once more, said with sickening charm: "Shall we?"

As he calmly invited Matt to accompany him, Mr Stovriec slightly turned his head. He threw the children a knowing look: the raised eyebrow, the sneering curl to his smile, told them all they needed to know.

Anthony and Destiny looked at each other glumly. Destiny's immediate horror had settled to a nauseating gripe in the pit of her stomach.

"It'll be OK," Anthony whispered, with far more conviction than he actually felt. Giving Destiny's arm a reassuring squeeze, Anthony smiled at her grimly. Then, with no other obvious alternative open to them, they followed the rapidly retreating figures of Anthony's dad and…

… not the man, Mr Stovriec, but the vindictive, ruthless and cruel Creation…

Crevitos!

# THANK YOU

Thank you for reading Emajen II, Saddler's Tale. I hope you lost yourself for just a little while in the fantasy worlds of Emajen and Doomland and Saddler's adventures there.

If you enjoyed reading this story, I would really appreciate it if you would leave a kind review on Amazon. Every review means a lot to me and helps other readers to find new books in the genres that they love.

Reviews do make a difference. YOUR review makes a difference to a book's success and helps to support your favourite authors.

Remember, every single reader makes writing a book worthwhile!

Follow me:

https://emajenblog.wordpress.com/

@ashleyledigo.bsky.social

Instagram @luvemajen

ACKNOWLEDGEMENTS

Thank you, as always, to my husband Tony for supporting me in everything I do. You are my rock, and I appreciate that fact every day.

Huge thanks go to my family, who tirelessly read everything I write and are always positive and creative with their constructive criticism.

I'm more grateful than you know.

COMING SOON

BERTHA BIGWORD & JIMMY JOLLY SAVE THE DAY

When their school is threatened by the appearance of a terrifying and elusive monster, Bertha and Jimmy decide to investigate. They need to find out what's going on, or all the children will leave, and their school might have to close forever!

Printed in Great Britain
by Amazon

54161601R00182